In Awesome Wonder

Bridging Science and Faith

— DANIEL RUY PEREIRA —

— LUIZ F. CARDOSO —

Sacristy Press
PO Box 612, Durham, DH1 9HT

www.sacristy.co.uk

First published in 2021 by Sacristy Press, Durham.

Sacristy Limited, registered in England & Wales, number 7565667

British Library Cataloguing-in-Publication Data
A catalogue record for the book is available from the British Library

ISBN 978-1-78959-148-4

Contents

Foreword

I met Daniel, Pastor Luiz and Dani Cardoso to discuss this project at a McDonald's in Oldham. Immediately, as they began to share their vision, it touched my heart and resonated so much with my own work in schools.

Seven years earlier I had been asked to demonstrate the compatibility of science and faith by the Anglican Diocese of Manchester, after the General Synod had voted overwhelmingly that science and faith were indeed compatible. Even though I was not a scientist myself, and had absolutely no science background, I readily accepted the challenge!

I founded a programme called "God and the Big Bang", which goes into schools for a day, with scientists of faith, to explore how science and faith come together. One element of the project is to research the attitudes of pupils; to do that we ask questions at the beginning of the day and ask the same questions again at the end of the day. What we found was stunning! After spending all their school years in an Anglican school, at the age of sixteen, 56 per cent of pupils said that science makes it hard to believe in God. We wanted to find out at what stage this issue manifested itself; we discovered that at the age of ten, 43 per cent of pupils in Anglican schools made the same statement. We eventually discovered that even before the age of ten years old, a lazy creationism appears to be being taught to pupils, without much consideration for its scientific or faith implications, which sets them up without much choice.

We found that teachers at primary level (five to eleven) often didn't realize that there were two creation stories in Genesis and multiple creation stories across the Bible and didn't know how to fit both science and faith together. This resulted in further research which found that only 27 per cent of pupils say that evolution and the biblical creation stories can both be true, and only 40 per cent said that science can support faith in God.

We also found that primary teachers were not aware that for most of Christian history, the early church fathers did not take Genesis as literal. Origen for example in the third century CE saw Genesis as a metaphor, writing:

> Who (thinks) that the first, and second, and third day, and the evening and the morning, existed without a sun, and moon, and stars? And that the first day was . . . without a sky. These things figuratively indicate certain mysteries . . . not literally.[1]

Or consider the thirteenth-century theologian and philosopher Thomas Aquinas, writing that God created potential:

> On the day God created the heaven and the earth, He also created every plant, not actually, but . . . potentially. All things were not distinguished together, not because God is not powerful . . . but so that things would be ordered.[2]

The way we teach both science and religious education at secondary level (from the age of eleven to eighteen) also compounds the issue of encouraging a false choice between science and faith. A lazy scientism begins with science taught as fact and proof, whereas religious education is taught and regarded as opinion. Religious studies teachers and science teachers rarely, if ever, teach the subjects together, despite science being in the religious studies curriculum; teachers tend not to want to attempt to answer a question in an area where they do not have subject knowledge. This gap between subjects further compounds the issue in that there are big questions at the nexus of both subject areas, so pupils are not given the chance to answer them.

This view of science and faith as fact and opinion respectively is not just in our schools but is also widespread in our societies. However, if you talk to scientists, they will tell you that most of their experiments fail, and that there is no such thing as absolute proof, but rather that there are probabilities, which can lead to the most marvellous new inventions, but which, nevertheless, remain as probabilities. So, there is always a hint of uncertainty, which prompts scientists to challenge everything and continue to improve their theories.

In listening to thousands of questions and almost hundreds of talks about faith and science, I have concluded as a non-scientist that science and faith are connected by mystery. For example, in science we do not know what dark matter is, but the fact that we do not know is the key to inspiring the science of the future. The value of science is that we are facing the unknown, and that is not to be feared but to be welcomed and embraced. Following the science means that we do not know the answers yet. Equally, in faith, we believe that our God is so powerful that we can never fully comprehend God's magnificence, but that means that our faith journey is about constant discovery. The value of faith is that we are also facing the unknown, we cannot anticipate tomorrow; the challenge of life is living with an uncertainty and a frailty that is not be feared but that is also to be welcomed and embraced. Following the faith also means that we do not know all the answers yet, and never will.

So, both science and faith can give us a sense of mystery and a sense of awe. Science helps us to amplify our view of the real, and our instruments help us amplify that reality. Those scientific instruments allow us to see some new territory, and so as we find out about the world, we start asking questions that we could not ask before. These questions are ones that we can't answer scientifically such as "Why is the speed of light that number?" The answer is that we simply don't know! The origin of the Universe is an open question, as is both the origin of life and the origin of consciousness. How do 85 billion neurons connected by the synapses give rise to who you are? Why do the constants of nature, such as the speed of light and the gravitational constant, amongst many others, have the value that they do? To paraphrase Einstein, the most fundamental emotion you can experience is the mysterious; it is the fundamental emotion at the cradle of science and the arts; the person who does not feel that is like a snuffed-out candle.[3]

Science has been one of humanity's greatest achievements. We live in an age of incredible scientific progress which has benefited all our lives, but there is more to discover. I love how Eugene Peterson, the author of the Message translation of the Bible, puts it in Proverbs 25:2: "God delights in concealing things; scientists delight in discovering things".

Science and faith have different jobs; science takes things apart to see how they work, and faith puts things together to see what they mean. Science is about how; faith is about why. Science tells us what is; faith tells us what ought to be. From faith comes a person's life purpose and from science, a person's possibility to achieve it. To understand life, you need science to interpret it, but you also need faith, for both are searching for the truth. Rabbi Jonathan Sacks, in an interview for his book *The Great Partnership: God, Science and the Search for Meaning*, quotes William Bragg: "Sometimes people ask if faith and science are not opposed to one another. They are in the sense that the thumb and fingers of my hands are opposed to one another. It is an opposition by means of which anything can be grasped."[4]

Recently when on holiday in Geneva, I visited CERN, where physicists are probing the fundamental structure of the Universe. Through instruments like the Large Hadron Collider, they are making particles collide together at close to the speed of light. But at the entrance to the Visitors Centre on the wall are three questions:

1. Where do we come from?
2. What is our place in the Universe?
3. Where are we going?

We have the capacity to wonder. We are the only creature alive that has this ability. It is not just our generation that has this ability, and we see this in the song book we call the Psalms.

There are no nature poems in the Psalms, only psalms in praise of the creator. Way before there were any concepts of ecosystems, the psalmists are joyous in the ordering of everything, in valleys and mountains; streams and rivers; sun, moon and stars; animals and human beings. But rather than praise the impersonal forces of nature the psalmists see them as being from the hand of God.

In Awesome Wonder, written by a teacher of science and a pastor/theologian, no less, comes at a time of great need to understand the compatibility of science and faith. You will find some thrilling science here which will expand your view of God. You will also discover that belief in God does not require a suspension of our critical thinking. You will come across the following extraordinary sentence:

> In the beginning, theologians were scientists and scientists were theologians, and they pondered the great works of God, and in them were delighted.

May we rediscover this close partnership within ourselves as scholars of both science and faith, and in that journey may we find that our faith is challenged, strengthened and deepened.

Michael Harvey
Executive Director, God and the Big Bang

Preface

The Church is a place where we learn stuff about God. His salvation plan, his characteristics and how to live a life that is worth living. It is also a safe space where we discuss various topics within the framework of a God-oriented world.

Unless, unfortunately, the topic is science that is.

Although many churches take upon themselves the task of talking about science, there is often ignorance. Or even enmity when one mentions science. Questioning is oftentimes suppressed somehow in younger or less-experienced Christians. As a result, many teenagers grow up with the assumption that Church and science are, indeed, enemies. In fact, people end up leaving the Church because of that.

But the Church is not the only one who does that. There is a widespread idea that great scientists of the past were revolutionaries against the oppressive Church. Those heroes were willing to burn on a stake for their "dangerous ideas" about the natural world. For some people, the Goliathan Church is still at odds with the poor Davidic science. And some of them spread ideas online, or on television and broadcasts.

As a science teacher, I see the result of both processes. My pupils ask me whether I believe in the Bible or in the Big Bang—as if those two must be exact opposite angles of a person's worldview.

One needs to remember, though, that opposite angles are equal. And in fact, when I return the question: "Why do I need to choose?", my pupils stagger. Then I proceed to tell them that science is another way to see the world. Another way of describing the behaviour of things God created a long time ago. When the smile comes forth, I add: "So I like both my Bible and my biology book!" They love it.

Inspired by this idea of a "war of worldviews", Pastor Luiz, a former atheist turned pastor, approached me, a former agnostic biology student turned Christian science teacher, to talk about a project of his. We would come up with an idea to answer questions that could be a stumbling stone for people to come to Church and hear the gospel. I liked that very much.

A few days later, though, he emailed me about an initiative called "Scientists in Congregation", organized by Templeton World Charity with St John's College at Durham University. We had some brainstorm meetings and applied for the grant with a simple proposition. We wanted to communicate how awesome the world is, and how we can perceive and do science for the glory of God. We would communicate that to our bilingual church, Connect Methodist Church, in the classical format of services. We would decorate the church with planets, balloons, periodic tables, and experiments for the children. As a Christian science teacher, I must confess, I went all out.

From January to July 2019, we had monthly meetings to polish our ideas and writing. We talked about our readings and answered some of each other's questions. I am sure those months will remain as some of the most fascinating I ever had in my Christian life.

The conversations we had reached their climax during October 2019, at Connect Methodist Church, in Stockport, in the series "In Awesome Wonder". Every service and discussion group would be science-oriented but seen from a biblical worldview. People engaged in the topics discussed. We sang a selection of songs about faith and science that would resonate with the sermon. People participated in experiments, cooked alien-shaped biscuits and got involved in social media. The children joined in of course, both with the experiments and with their lessons in Sunday school. I still remember the eyes of boys and girls when I extracted DNA from the cheek-cells of Dani Cardoso, our worship leader and one of the three co-directors of the project, herself a psychologist. And the conversation about UFO sightings in our coffee area after Session 4 with Fernanda was memorable.

In the services, the focus was the sermon. Pastor Luiz and I felt it would be more profitable to our community to present the ideas in a classical church-style. I would preach in English; he would translate to Portuguese. Thank God, it worked. The many conversations, two baptisms and the interest our community developed for science in the following months are a good sign. We even changed our coffee area, replacing (most of the time) plastic cups for paper cups. There is room for progress, though.

This book is the product of the whole experience.

We would like to thank our families for their support and apologize for our disappearance during those months where we were so focused on the project. We thank Templeton World Charity Foundation and St John's College's "Scientists in Congregation" initiative, without which this wonderful part of our lives would not have happened.

Above all, we thank our community at Connect Methodist Church, who embraced the idea and, just like us, went all out to learn about our Creator God and his Creation.

Daniel Ruy Pereira
Oldham, 2020

CHAPTER 1

God's awesome Universe

For what can be known about God is plain to them, because God has shown it to them. For his invisible attributes, namely, his eternal power and divine nature, have been clearly perceived, ever since the creation of the world, in the things that have been made. So they are without excuse.

Romans 1:19–20

We have known about the sphericality of Earth for centuries. But the place it occupies in the Universe only started to become clear during the twentieth century. Until the work of astronomer Edwin Hubble was published, scientists believed that the cosmos was very much smaller, but in fact, in that time the Universe was only our galaxy—the Milky Way.

In Genesis 15:5, God says to Abraham: "Look toward heaven, and number the stars, if you are able to number them". Back in those days, there was neither light nor atmospheric pollution that could hamper Abraham's vista. Those who live in the biggest metropolis can barely grasp what the patriarch's eyes would have captured. However, using computer programs, we could simulate that!

On the software *Stellarium* one can set up a night sky observation back to 1 January 2091 BC. That could have been the year in which Abraham would have moved over to Canaan.[5]

Figure 1: Abraham stargazes, in obedience to God. As he does that, focused on God's promises, he has no idea of the complexities and wonder those luminous dots would bring us, centuries later.

Supposing he was looking above just halfway between the horizon and the zenith, around 8.00pm, he would have seen more stars than we can see today close to cities.

That is only possible because the Universe God created is full of regularities. We know the position of the stars today and tomorrow, so we assume that the galaxy will not descend into unpredictable chaos overnight. Computer software can make such a prediction based on equations developed by scientists, delivering a precise simulation we can rely on.

A dark night, especially in winter and far from cities, reveals many stars with different luminosity levels, sometimes organized in specific patterns. In January, looking East, you can see "Orion's belt", three stars in a line, in the Orion constellation. In that constellation, on the top left-hand side, there is a bright red star, called Betelgeuse. It is between 642 and 724 light-years away from us. It shines against what appears to be a cloudy background. But that is no cloud. It is, actually, one of the arms of the Milky Way, the galaxy in which we live.

All the stars you see with a naked eye when you stargaze are in the Milky Way alone, which is 100,000 light-years across and contains something around 100 billion stars.[6]

Our galaxy is part of a galaxy cluster called the Local Group, numbering more than 50 galaxies. One of them is Andromeda, which is moving fast towards the Milky Way. Be careful if you are still here in 4 billion years!

Figure 2 shows the first picture of Andromeda, photographed by Isaac Roberts in 1899. When he took the photo, nobody imagined Andromeda was another galaxy. Today we know there are other galaxies, and we estimate their number to be more than 2 trillion—each one of them housing billions of stars.

The numbers you have read on the last two pages are so immense that we can only try and comprehend them if we use some day-to-day comparisons. For example, imagine stars are all the same size as oranges (although they greatly vary in size).

If our sun were about that size, left on the floor, in Manchester, the Earth would be the size of a grain of sand about 1 millimetre across, 20 metres away from the sun. But the closest star, Proxima Centauri, would

Figure 2: Andromeda galaxy, by Isaac Roberts, 1899,
from his book *A Selection of Photographs of Stars, Star-
clusters and Nebulae, Volume II*. Nowadays, we can see the
same galaxy with much more detail and colour, through
instruments such as the Hubble Space Telescope.

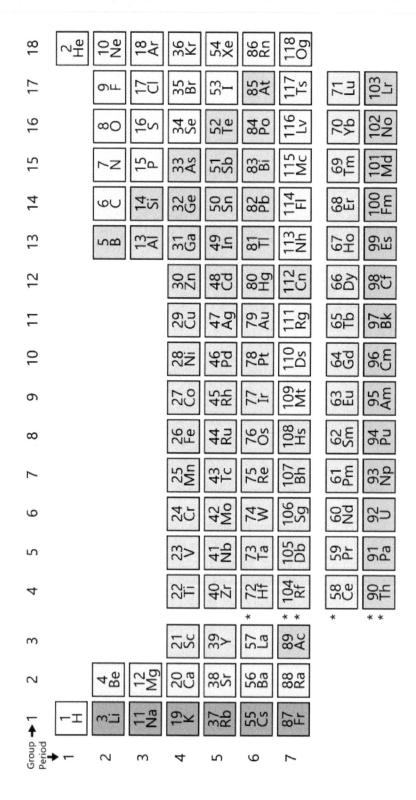

be as far as São Paulo, Brazil, more than 10,000 kilometres away. Other stars would be where the sun and planets are *in real life*.[7]

Only light can travel those vast distances because it has the top speed in our Universe. One light-year is the distance light travels in one year, at 300,000 km/s, which is equal to 9,460,000,000,000 km. Imagine you were able to travel out in the cosmos at the national speed limit (70 miles per hour in Britain), never stopping nor changing your speed. It would "only" take you more than 98 million years to cover that distance! But a beam of light does that in a single year. Hence, a light-year. Should you wish to travel over to Proxima Centauri, 4.2 light-years away from us, it would take you more than 390 million years to get there. More if you wanted to do regular stops for the interstellar toilets!

Now, imagine trying to travel across the Milky Way, 100,000 light-years across. And ours is a relatively small galaxy among billions of galaxies.

Faced with such "astronomical" distances, many people ask why would God need to create a universe so ridiculously immense? Well, it turns out it has all to do with the periodic table of elements, which almost any GCSE student can explain to you—probably incorrectly!

Relevant to our discussion here are the elements represented by the numbers 6, 7, 8 and 9, primarily C (carbon)—the fundamental element that life as we know it is made up of. Every kind of living thing described so far (about 1.5 million species[8]) is made up of carbon atoms, including their proteins, DNA, sugars and fat. But carbon, as well as the other elements, is forged in the unimaginable temperatures of the stars:

> When the core hydrogen of a big star is completely converted into helium . . . its nucleus is pressed inwards, squeezed hotter and hotter until helium itself starts reacting . . . When that helium

Figure 3: The Periodic Table of Elements, as of 2020. In this table are represented all known elements in the Universe, in order of increasing properties, such as number of protons inside their nuclei, number of atomic mass and how many energy "shells" there are in each atom. It is astonishing that we can represent the building blocks of the Universe in a table, ordered by their properties.

is used up, the star continues contracting and warming up even more ... They then emit more energy via the production of carbon (with six protons) and then, progressively heavier nuclei: oxygen, neon, sodium, silicon etc.[9]

The Universe must be more than 13 billion years old so that massive stars like those described above by Sir Martin Rees could form. Consequently, it had to be immense and boiling with galaxies all over. Otherwise, there would be no life on earth—simply because carbon, iron, sodium and other elements wouldn't exist. The size of the Universe and the number of stars is *providential*.

Now, keep those numbers and hard science facts in mind, right next to the word "providential".

God is infinite in creativity; therefore, it makes sense that his creation (Psalm 8) is also immense and creative. He created the Universe for himself, for his glory and enjoyment, leaving in it traces of his nature—as an artist would do. But in one of those stars, back in the Milky Way galaxy, God put a star 500 times smaller than Betelgeuse. We call it the sun. That star is the one we see every day, when we look up, and which the Indian sage Sadhu Sundar Singh used to express his understanding of the Trinity:

> I [Jesus] and the Father and the Holy Spirit are One. Just as in the Sun there are both heat and light, but the light is not heat, and the heat is not light, but both are one, though in their manifestation they have different forms, so I and the Holy Spirit, proceeding from the Father, bring light and heat to the world. . . . I who am the True Light, dissipate all dark and evil desires . . . Yet We are not three but One, just as the Sun is but one.[10]

This analogy is only possible because of the nature of the Universe God created. If God is the Creator, and the Universe is his creation, one would expect that his work would display some of his traits, like providence and the Trinity, for example. These are easily detectable if we only know some essential characteristics of God. Similarly, a beautiful dress evokes the name of its stylist. You only have to be familiar with his or her work to identify the dress as his or her making.

In Romans 1:19–20, Paul writes in the middle of the first century to a church he never visited before. He appeals precisely to this argument to build up his idea of humans being inexcusable before God. On the last day, we will not be able to say we never saw signs of his presence in the world, or even his characteristics. The apostle argues that God can be apprehended (known) in the Universe (the "created things"). He wants to be seen in the Universe. Therefore, the cosmos somehow points straight up to its creator.

Christians see in that the perfect motivation to transform their vision of God, world and life, and then to worship God in a unique language as they learn about the natural world.

God can be perceived in the Universe

Some people see science as an enemy of faith; something cunning ready to choke religion at the faintest sign of frailty. As if science were the Big Bad Wolf hunting the innocent little red-hooded girl as she goes to Grandma's house singing hymns.

Well, they are downright wrong, Paul would argue. "Whatever can be known from God is clear to them."

The problem here is not in the clarity of the natural phenomena. It lies in the human confusion which is trying to impose its way of seeing reality on to our favourite form of understanding the world (including a Christian vision of the world). For theologian Justo L. González, no one has ever proved nor denied the existence of God through science for a straightforward reason:

> What matters to us about creation is not how the world was made but who made it. . . . The Bible is not primarily about the how but about the who and the for what . . . [11]

Science, however, must deal with facts—be that describing, explaining or predicting. When it goes beyond facts, it betrays its nature and loses credibility. This happens, for instance, when scientists claim that the beginning of life arose by pure chance or by God. There is no way that either can ever be observed, proved, or disproved. They do not even provide a particularly useful hypothesis. When it comes to the origin of the world and of humankind, science may be very good at suggesting the *how* but has no scientific way to explain, affirm, or deny the *who* or the *for what*.[12]

It is not the role of science to answer questions about a *supernatural* being since it only deals with *natural* phenomena. However, the same natural events, curiously, point to specific characteristics of the Universe that reflect the work of God in its creation.

For example, the Bible presents God as the Lawgiver. He is the one who creates laws so his people can distinguish themselves from other ungodly people. And also themselves pure, functioning as a holy society. The servant of God (and, in fact, the whole world even if it doesn't serve him) is obliged to obey various inescapable laws—such as gravity.

Even more impressive is our mysterious ability to describe and apply those laws in an appropriate language—the language of mathematics.

One of the most mysterious phenomena of the Universe, gravity, is still not fully understood. Even with our embarrassing difficulties, we know it is a force. Possibly a kind of particle. Maybe both. The point is: gravity is present in every corner of the Universe. It is responsible both for the origin and destiny of the cosmos, the maintenance of the planets' translation (their orbit around the sun) and keeping celestial bodies locked in their galaxies. On the ground level, gravity is the force that keeps us, literally, down to earth.

Gravity is also an *invisible* force. So much so that, for about 200 years, humanity was convinced that it operated just as Sir Isaac Newton said. But in the twentieth century, Albert Einstein showed that Newton's idea of gravity works well in small, daily objects as well as in big objects up to a point, such as stars and planets, but that there could be particular objects in space (black holes, as we know them nowadays) where gravity would operate mysteriously. Or, as the Standard Model of Quantum Physics shows, breaks down completely in the subatomic world. *Mysteriously.*

To wrap this up for our purposes: gravity is a law, clearly described and applied via language (mathematics). It is invisible. It is eternal, in the sense that it has existed since the beginning of the Universe and it will continue to be there until its end. It is a mysterious force. What a divine thing gravity is!

The Universe (*kosmos*, in Greek) is full of laws like that. We could talk about the law of conservation of masses, where, in a chemical reaction, none of the masses of the reactants is lost or created, but all is conserved in the new products that form. It is a *maintaining* law. So, if a plant uses a certain mass of carbon dioxide and water, it will produce (through photosynthesis) the same mass, in glucose and oxygen. Again, if this law were not present since the beginning of the Universe, life on earth would not be possible. Without photosynthesis, there would be no oxygen in the concentration we have in the atmosphere we breathe, and there would be no glucose, the basis of any food. The law of conservation of masses rules the products in the Universe.

From the Big Bang until the end of times, gravity, the speed of light, the law of conservation of masses and many other natural laws have been ruling the Universe. Similarly to God, they are "eternal" because they have always been present in our Universe. Since we can express those laws in a mathematical language (in words), they also show divine nature. You would do well to recollect what John says in the first sentence of his Gospel: "In the beginning was the Word, and the Word was with God, and the Word was God" (John 1:1).

God not only wanted his Universe to display his attributes, though. He wants much more than that.

God wants to be known in the Universe

In every laboratory, every scientist works in their area of expertise, be it biology, chemistry, physics or any of the expansive sub-disciplines. These are highly qualified professionals, working on the next discovery or technology for the betterment of human life. Maybe he or she will come up with new medicines, better aero-spatial technology, effective treatment for a disease or the development of new vaccines. But deep inside, every scientist is still a young child fascinated by the complexity of a part of the Universe.

The astrophysicist Neil deGrasse Tyson once said:

> When I think of science, and of the scientists, I think of children
> that never lost the curiosity and wonder and so, one day, woke
> up as adults with the same feeling of searching for that which is
> true and untrue in this world.[13]

We hear echoes, in the back of our heads, of the words of Jesus in Matthew 19:14: "Let the little children come to me and do not hinder them, for to such belongs the kingdom of heaven." The same children marvel before the night sky and stand in awe before the complexities of a cell seen in a microscope. The same children spend their afternoons watching videos and documentaries about nature. They can look up to Jesus and marvel, intrigued, in a similar way. After all, you read the stories and hear of Jesus healing blind people without medicine or treatment, see him transforming water into wine, or hear of him coming back from the dead—without defibrillators! You see him *redeeming* creation.

Curiosity, perseverance and wonder often lead us to fascinating places. One can look up some images taken by the Hubble Space Telescope (HST), for example, and find the galaxy Messier 51 (Figure 4), or M51, in the constellation of Canes Venatici. Many pictures were taken of that galaxy but one of them, from its nucleus, shows a curious (and unusual) detail, seen in Figure 5.

We see an "x" or a "cross" depending on the angle that is created by the absorption of dust, marking the exact position of a black hole, whose mass can be equivalent to a million suns, and a diameter of 1,100 light-years. There are many other interesting facts in the image, but the illustration for us is undeniable.

The creator, through precise-working laws of space and time, managed to create a black hole in the middle of a galaxy, which is beautiful to our eyes. Why we find it beautiful or can even describe it and, to some extent, explain it, is a mystery. But we do. Moreover, we needed a powerful telescope such as the Hubble to capture it. Throughout history, we had to invent and improve on the telescope so we could *satisfy our search*. When its light reaches our eyeballs though, it displays a dark cross in a halo, coming from a remote past. In our brains and hearts, we recall that

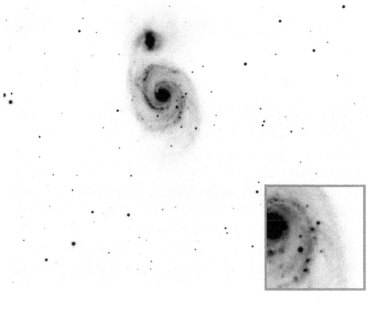

Figure 4: Spiral galaxy M51, where new stars are forming. The filter has been changed to negative.

Figure 5: "X" Structure in the nucleus of galaxy M51.

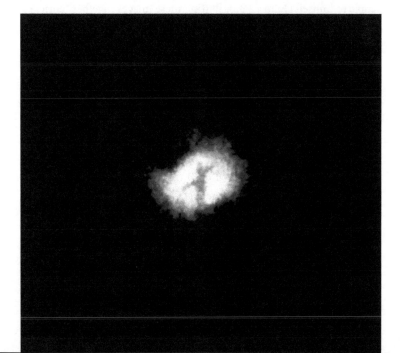

we were saved by Jesus Christ, who became "obedient to death—even death on a cross!" (Philippians 2:8, NIV). "He was chosen before the creation of the world, but was revealed in these last times for your sake" (1 Peter 1:20, NIV).

The smile is inevitable.

Of course, such an analysis of the image is utterly unnecessary; it is not even a tiny bit scientific and is subject to a Christian, Trinitarian worldview of reality.[14] It is, perhaps, even *childish* in a good way—being evocative of the curious and wondering child in us. And that is precisely the point! The Christian can appreciate a hard, dry, data-loaded image such as this (a black hole sucking up dust like a colossal hoover) as a pointer to the intentions and plans of our Creator.

God wants to be perceived and known in his Universe. Much like artists put their flair into their paintings, God wants people to look at his creation and remember him, his work and his attributes. But also, our failures, that we are dust, and that he worked for our redemption. The nucleus of galaxy M51 might be only a dust-sucking black hole, but it resembles a cross, and in that symbol, there is sin, punishment, justice, mercy and grace; there is the infinite love of God and the infinite injustice of humanity created in his image, and there is Christ, the light of the world, who, like a black hole, when lifted from the earth, will draw all people to himself (John 12:32). Putting these images together "enriches one's perception of reality", as Alister McGrath says, giving us back the joy of curiosity and wonder of creation.[15]

The Universe points to God

Paul does not use creation as proof of the existence of God; neither should we. When people try to do that, that approach proves to be inefficient and unfruitful. Francis Collins, director of the incredible Human Genome Project that mapped the entire human DNA (concluded in 2003), defends that one should not use God to fill gaps in our knowledge:

> A word of caution is needed when inserting specific divine action
> by God in this or any other area where scientific understanding

is currently lacking. From solar eclipses in older times to the movement of the planets in the Middle Ages to the origins of life today, this "God of the gaps" approach has all too often done a disservice to religion (and by implication, to God, if that's possible). . . . There are good reasons to believe in God, including the existence of mathematical principles and order in creation. They are positive reasons, based on knowledge, rather than default assumptions based on (a temporary) lack of knowledge.[16]

The truth is that the Bible itself defends a faith without any scientific proof. Well, it would not be faith if evidence was available, as warns the writer of Hebrews: "faith is the assurance of things *hoped for*, the conviction of things *not seen*" (Hebrews 11:1, our emphasis). Again, the apostle Paul emphasizes that point in 1 Corinthians 1:18–25:

> For the word of the cross is *folly* to those who are perishing, but to us who are being saved it is the power of God. For it is written,
>
> "I will destroy the wisdom of the wise,
> and the discernment of the discerning I will thwart."
>
> Where is the one who is wise? Where is the scribe? Where is the debater of this age? Has not God made foolish the wisdom of the world? For since, in the wisdom of God, the world did not know God through wisdom, *it pleased God through the folly of what we preach to save those who believe*. For Jews demand signs and Greeks seek wisdom, but we preach Christ crucified, a stumbling block to Jews and folly to Gentiles, but to those who are called, both Jews and Greeks, Christ the power of God and the wisdom of God. For the foolishness of God is wiser than men, and the weakness of God is stronger than men. (our emphasis)

God doesn't want to press the unbeliever against the wall, yelling: "Behold the proof and repent, thou cursed sinner!" Many people would like God to be like that, but that would be idolatry, since the true God is not like that at all. He is the creator, but also the redeemer. He became dust like us, to be sucked in to the black hole of our sin but, through his cross, we can see light and beauty, in the horror of crucifixion and the glory of his resurrection. All of that because he loves us.

Scientists and theologians sometimes explain some of the Universe's mysteries. But most of the time they are equally baffled by the same questions. Especially when they, "in awesome wonder, consider all the works His hands have made".[17]

There are no excuses

The Universe is mysterious, but, as scientists believe, it can be described and explained without the need for the concept of God the Creator. However, we firmly believe that it cannot be *comprehended in full* without God. Alister McGrath, originally a biochemist who later became a theologian, phrases it well:

> . . . though I loved science as a young man, I had a sense that it wasn't complete. Science helped me to understand how things worked. But what did they mean? Science gave me a neat answer to the question of how I came to be in this world. Yet it seemed unable to answer a deeper question. Why was I here? What was the point of life?[18]

Christ can provide a definite answer to those questions, which are phrased differently in the life story of each one of us. Gravity, so strong in some objects, so negligible in others, not only determines the Universe as we have it, but also allows you to relax under the shadow of an apple tree, thinking about why you are here. Likewise, God is not only seen in the Universe, explaining and enriching reality, but he also offers answers to those who seek them.

We can study the *cosmos* because of the natural order and regularity it displays. We can describe it in language, through parables or figures of speech, because it is ruled by identifiable, predictable laws, to which all living things are inescapably subject.

The Universe is full of structures that appeal directly to human curiosity, often leaving us in awe when beholding its power and mystery. But some structures point to the attributes of God and the redemptive work of Jesus Christ. Precisely because of that, they offer an extra richness to our vision of reality, so much so that one can perceive God, clearly, in the "created things".

There are no excuses not to think about God when studying nature through science, but one can make many excuses about not surrendering, even after being presented with so many pointers.

CHAPTER 2

Science and faith in fellowship

The heavens declare the glory of God,
and the sky above proclaims his handiwork.
Day to day pours out speech,
and night to night reveals knowledge.
There is no speech, nor are there words,
whose voice is not heard.
Their voice goes out through all the earth,
and their words to the end of the world.

Psalm 19:1–4

Great are the works of the Lord,
studied by all who delight in them.

Psalm 111:2

Scotland is home to the highest mountain in the British Isles: the legendary Ben Nevis. One of the favourite destinations of those who enjoy hiking, Ben Nevis is known for being quite a bizarre mountain. Figure 6 shows why: it offers a different experience depending on where one starts hiking.

Imagine that two climbers take part in an experiment. They are blindfolded and taken by a helicopter to Ben Nevis, where they are parachuted, each onto one of the two different sides of the mountain, at

Figure 6: In this drawing by Rachael Ayers (2021), both faces of Ben Nevis, in Scotland, can be seen. One of them is rough and difficult to climb, but the other is smoother.

its base. They take away the blindfold and walk up. All is new to them, but they start climbing, describing, in their reports, the vista as they go.

Eventually, both reach the peak at different times.

One asks the other: "So how was it?"

The south-side climber says: "Oh, it was fine—a lot of green and grass. I had quite a relaxed time. What about you?"

The other climber, sceptical, says: "Buddy, are you joking? It was horrible. I have never seen such a dangerous, rocky mountain in all my life!"

Now, staring at each other, three possibilities cross their minds. The first scenario has each of them fighting to the death to defend its description of the mountain. The second has them soaking it in and never talking to each other ever again. The third scenario has them sitting down, having a cup of tea and try learning from each other about the different landscape that they each experienced.[19]

Which possibility would you choose?

Many in the world today, it seems, would rather fight to the death.

We see and experience the different aspects of creation from various points of view. On the one hand, theologians seek to help Christians to try to understand the challenges of life and its harsh realities. That is one side of the mountain. On the other hand, scientists do the same thing to the other side, but the landscape is a bit different. We are not even considering the other climbers: artists, philosophers, poets, teachers, children, elderly etc.

Everyone has a vision of how the world is and how it ought to be. One uses specific languages to describe the reality one seeks to understand. A lot of that experience is lost in translation, though. Somebody who gazes at the mountain in a photo book cannot comprehend the real dimensions of it. Therefore, one needs another's expertise to build a better understanding of the world; so goes the quote attributed to the physicist James Joule:

> It is evident that an acquaintance with natural laws means no less than an acquaintance with the mind of God therein expressed.[20]

In the twentieth century, the Church has been undecided and split concerning God's creation. Many Christians and scientists stare at the mountain (nature) from a distance, satisfied with that little experience of it, but without accessing a complete description, or without taking up the task of climbing up and down from different starting points.

Often, this is because Christians and scientists do not really want to talk to each other. But when they do, if they do take up the challenge, they will see a beautiful mountain. It is complex, being both easy and hard, fair and ugly, high and small. A truth which is recalled by the graven message on the tombstone of the microbiologist Louis Pasteur, a devout Catholic, at the Pasteur Institute in Paris:

> Happy the man who bears within him a divinity, an ideal of
> beauty and obeys it; an ideal of art, an ideal of science, an ideal
> of country, and an ideal of the virtues of the Gospel.[21]

He was right. One needs only to climb the mountain, as proposed by the writers of Psalm 19 and Psalm 111. The act of praising God includes not only an acknowledgement of who he is but also an understanding of the extent of his work. They invite the reader to look at creation with the eyes of worship and to spend their days wondering, thinking and delighting in creation. But just as the scientist needs a method, so do we!

So, we offer a method which will sound familiar both to the Christian and to the scientist that have decided to climb up the mountain. The Psalmist offers them three indispensable tools for the climb. These tools ought to be in the backpack, as they provide theological, scientific, and psychological support.

Recognize that God's works are great

Steve Lawson argues that the expression "works of God" in the Bible almost always refers to the creation, and such is the case in Psalm 111:2.[22] What the writer has in mind is the works of God in the natural world.

In antiquity, knowledge concerning the natural world was quite limited and always associated with gods and goddesses. In fact, the notion of the absence of God (or gods) was pretty much unthinkable (see more in Chapter 5).

We take current knowledge for granted because, since we were very young, we were taught it in school. So, we don't question some stuff, such as the body being made up of cells. We don't doubt that we all came from a single cell, the product of the fusion of a sperm cell and an egg cell in our mother's uterus (womb); but that knowledge is recent—not older than 150 years old. Our understanding of DNA is not even a century old, and it has advanced much since 2003, when scientists concluded the Human Genome Project. By the way, all sciences change and carry on changing. They rewrite themselves as we unveil new facts or come up with new theories that allow us to improve our explanation (and detection via new instruments) of natural phenomena.

In that sense, good theories would not be very different from Rocky Balboa. They keep being punched harder and harder but always stand up and win at the end of the challenge. After all, theories that wouldn't stand up fail to endure.

The Psalmist's wonder is not exclusive to himself. We share that wonder when we observe protists in a drop of pondwater, or when we study human anatomy. The realization that a snail contains the two sexes in its body is fascinating. How marvelled are we when we see robots and probes going on interplanetary trips? The scientist experiences the same thrill of the grandeur of our Universe. Carl Sagan (an agnostic astrophysicist), one of the greatest writers of popular science, television presenter and active participant in NASA's space programme, wrote:

> Not only is science compatible with spirituality; it is also a profound source of spirituality. When we recognize our place in the immensity of light-years and the passage of aeons, when we face the complexity, beauty and subtlety of life, then that growing feeling, that sense of euphoria and humbleness combined, that is certainly of spiritual nature.[23]

Some people are not satisfied with that feeling though. They understand the experience is more than spiritual, pointing to something beyond, as we argued in Chapter 1.

John Polkinghorne (1930–2021) was a successful theoretical physicist who exchanged his academic career for a pastoral ministry in the Anglican Church, and he says:

> Our rational faculties are very important, and their exercise can save us from all sorts of folly. However, we are a great deal more than minds, and a real view of the world will have to engage our whole personalities. That is why religions always speak of an act of faith, a response at the deepest levels of our being to that One who is the ground of our being. In the end, a religious view of the world is not a philosophical attitude but a personal commitment. Some form of a leap of faith is inevitable. I do not think that it is a question of shutting our eyes and hoping for the best in a blind lunge at reality. Of course, we should look before we leap. Faith cannot be proved, but it is not unmotivated.[24]

Science starts with curiosity, and it often comes with surprising wonder. What are those luminous dots in the sky? Are they gods or can they be explained naturally? How does a seed transform into a tree? Is it a goddess or a complex biological process? What is the job of cells? Where does the oxygen that we breathe come from? What determines that my brother has my mother's eyes, but I take after my father, who has brown eyes? Those questions come up almost out of nowhere, but not quite. They come with and from the feeling that the Universe is enormous and curious.

Ponder God's complex works

After realizing that the works of God are great, the Psalmist says that the individual should "ponder" them. The original word can be translated as "meditate", or "think about them carefully", "one is occupied with certain things and then wonders about them". Surely throughout history, people understood the term, "ponder", in different ways, but with the advance of science, it has become a lot more of a challenge to "ponder" creation without employing certain scientific methods.

The main reason that we have the lifestyle which we have today is the scientific development of society. Centuries of inventions and tinkering have brought us to where we find ourselves today. For example, would it be possible to imagine a world without television, computers or smartphones which can access the internet on the go? Is it possible to imagine modern medicine without the microscope or the pharmaceutical industry? Would our banking systems be possible without computers? What about the exponential increment of the power of microscopy? What made in vitro fertilization (IVF) possible? Why do we have relatively cheap dental treatments and public health systems?

All those advancements are made possible by certain methods and thought processes used to answer questions. We ended up calling that "science".

Unfortunately, many churches fail to recognize that; but one needs only to go into one of these churches and observe the service. How many scientific products are to be found within the very church preaching against the achievements of science?

Preachers use microphones (product of the field of acoustics). Some of them might use glasses or contact lenses (ophthalmology). The presentation of the main points of a sermon often has the aid of an electronic projector connected to a modern laptop (computer science and optics). Churchgoers, moved by the sermon, post some quotes on social media. Their smartphones automatically recognize the devices' location via GPS, which would not exist without Einstein's theory of general relativity. Even the Bibles, when not printed using modern machinery, are digital in e-readers, phones or tablets. And most go to the church using their hi-tech cars, taking their repeat prescription before and after the service!

Science is here to stay, and it is a useful way to ponder the works of God, a true blessing. But how did it begin? According to Ernst Mayr, one of the most prominent biologists of the twentieth century, modern science started in a period of history he calls the "scientific revolution":

> Virtually all architects of the Scientific Revolution remained devout Christians, however, and, not surprisingly, the kind of science they created was very much a branch of the Christian

faith. In this view, the world was created by God, and thus it could not be chaotic. It was governed by his laws, which, because they were God's laws, were universal. . . . The task of God's science, then, was to find these universal laws, to find the ultimate truth of everything as embodied in these laws, and to test their truth by way of predictions and experiments.[25]

So, scientific thought flowed partially from the Christian praxis, as an extension of an act of worship, which could not be avoided by those whose minds were too curious to be quiet. The eighteenth-century founder of Methodism, John Wesley, was interested in (and wrote about) science.

In the beginning, theologians were scientists and scientists were theologians, and they pondered the great works of God, and in them were delighted.

Precisely because of that, one of the significant gifts of the Church to science was to set it free to be practised by those who did not share the same faith. After all, creation is God's work and can be described by a human being, religious or not. It's no wonder that the description (after careful proofreading and scrutinizing by other scientists) highlights the works of God. It is not at all surprising that it imparts such awe over the most curious scientific fact.

However, the Christian sees that without God to give an extra meaning to hard, dry numbers, graphs and diagrams of the scientific papers, only one side of the mountain is in focus. Alister McGrath says it beautifully:

> Christian theology is the elixir, the philosopher's stone, which turns the mundane into the epiphanic, the world of nature into the realm of God's creation. Like a lens bringing a vast landscape into sharp focus, or a map helping us grasp the features of the terrain around us, Christian doctrine offers a new way of understanding, imagining, and behaving. It invites us to see the natural order, and ourselves within it, in a special way—a way that might be hinted at, but cannot be confirmed by, the natural order itself.[26]

The perception that science and religion (especially the Christian faith) are in a state of war is but a distortion—looking to one side of the mountain, claiming it to be the whole picture. That is, in all honesty, nonsense.

Many scientists testify that the reality of a scientific praxis solidly based upon a robust Christian faith "runs instead of being lame"—to paraphrase Albert Einstein. It allows one to climb the mountain faster, covering more of its facets. According to Max Planck, Nobel Prize winner in Physics in 1918:

> There can never be any real opposition between Religion and Science; for the one is the complement of the other. Every serious and reflective person realizes, I think, that the religious element in his nature must be recognized and cultivated if all the powers of the human soul are to act together in perfect balance and harmony. And indeed it was not by any accident that the greatest thinkers of all ages were also deeply religious souls, even though they made no public show of their religious feeling. It is from the cooperation of the understanding with the will that the finest fruit of philosophy has arisen, namely, the ethical fruit. Science enhances the moral values of life, because it furthers a love of truth and reverence—love of truth displaying itself in the constant endeavour to arrive at a more exact knowledge of the world of mind and matter around us, and reverence, because every advance in knowledge brings us face to face with the mystery of our own being.[27]

In other words, it is an absolute delight to study God's great works.

The climber's chief aim is to reach the mountain's peak so it can appreciate the world from the mountain top. After all the hard work, dedication, and effort to conquer the summit, the climber sits down, rests and admires the outcome of the climb. Not unlike the scientist who discovers something new and has that unique, infinitesimal joy; or the Christian who understands one aspect of God in his or her own life.

The pilot of the lunar module of the Apollo 15 mission, James B. Irwin, who spent almost three days on the moon (with David R. Scott, whilst

Figure 7: James Irwin and the Lunar Roving
Vehicle during the Apollo 15 mission.

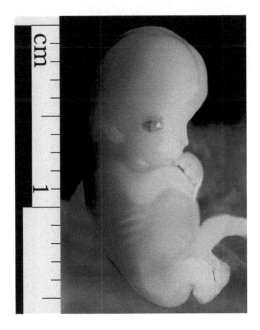

Figure 8: Human
embryo, at
seven weeks of
development,
about 1.5 cm long.
Photo by Andrzej
Zachwieja and
Jan Walczewski.

Alfred M. Worden stayed in the Command Module),[28] returned to his Christian faith after returning from space and said:

> The Earth reminded us of a Christmas tree ornament hanging in the blackness of space. As we got farther and farther away it diminished in size. Finally it shrank to the size of a marble, the most beautiful marble you can imagine. That beautiful, warm, living object looked so fragile, so delicate, that if you touched it with a finger it would crumble and fall apart. Seeing this has to change a man, has to make a man appreciate the creation of God and the love of God.[29]

Irwin is the alpinist who climbed the highest possible peak and had the privilege of a wholesome vista. From there, he saw that the mountain has more than one side. He realized that, although he had successfully climbed one side, using the tools and languages appropriate to that side, there was a whole new world to explore.

God's presence in creation is worthy of exploration

The Bible is full of stories like that of Irwin. Not only when one is looking up, like in Psalm 19, but also when one looks inside, towards our development, nowadays described and explained by the sciences of embryology, biochemistry and others. But there was nothing even close when David wrote Psalm 139:

> For you formed my inward parts;
> you knitted me together in my mother's womb.
> I praise you, for I am fearfully and wonderfully made.
> Wonderful are your works;
> my soul knows it very well.
> My frame was not hidden from you,
> when I was being made in secret,
> intricately woven in the depths of the earth.
> Your eyes saw my unformed substance;

in your book were written, every one of them,
the days that were formed for me,
when as yet there was none of them.

The expression "unformed substance" can nowadays be translated to "embryo". David is describing, jaw-dropped, the mystery of a baby's development. Nowadays we know a lot about embryonic development—still, it is beautiful and awe-inspiring. Even if somebody takes God away from the process, as embryologist Jamie Davies does in the following quote, the awe and wonder are still present, although not satisfied:

Understanding more about how we got here, about the astonishing processes by which we constructed ourselves, only adds to the respect and awe with which we can view the creation of each human being, whether a stranger, a friend, or our own, unique, self-made self.[30]

But when one thinks that God chose to become one of those embryos, going through the same "knitting" that the creatures made in his image go through, that is even more astonishing:

And when I think of God, His Son not sparing
Sent Him to die, I scarce can take it in
That on the Cross, my burden gladly bearing
He bled and died to take away my sin
Then sings my soul, my Saviour God, to Thee
How great Thou art, How great Thou art.[31]

Even only superficial knowledge of the complexity of our development and growth is enough to baffle any scholar before the biological might of a living cell. The more we discover, the more mysteries we find. But not to seek to unveil the secret is like stopping the climb halfway through, only to gaze at the top, presuming that it is beautiful but never going there—having given up.

The Psalmist and the astronaut have the same attitude, though: in their ways, they praise him, for they were fearfully and wonderfully made!

At the summit

Christians are the pilgrims who climb the mountain and journey towards the "Celestial City", as John Bunyan would have it. Scientists are the climbers striving to conquer the mountain for the pleasure and satisfaction this achievement would bring them. Both use specific tools and languages to climb each mountainside—the Universe where we live.

But, if scientists would do well in remembering that they can climb through the path of science and come back through the path of faith, Christians would do well to remember that the route can be taken the other way around. Both fail when they don't get together to offer God the praise due to him.

In our story, though, there is a very happy ending. Both climbers sit down together at the peak of Ben Nevis, eat bread, drink wine, and celebrate Holy Communion.

**Figure 9: "Two climbers, One World",
Khelvi Marques, 2020, for this book.**

CHAPTER 3

Evolution in Christian life

> Count it all joy, my brothers, when you meet trials of various kinds, for you know that the testing of your faith produces steadfastness. And let steadfastness have its full effect, that you may be perfect and complete, lacking in nothing.
>
> *James 1:2–4*

I recall having a biology-filled childhood. My dad always liked gardening, and he cared for a small garden in our backyard. My brother and I used to spend a lot of time there, especially me, studying plants, ants, woodlice, slugs and earthworms. My favourite animals were the ants, although I think they did not share the love.

Eventually, I made my mind up, that I would henceforth teach the big ants in my backyard to swim because I thought that if they wanted to survive the cruel world, such a skill would be fundamental! So, with a charity-filled soul, using a peg, I would peg up some ants from the steady line in which they were marching, and I would drop them into a bucket full of water. I could not understand why they would stop moving, but I would notice the others, undisturbed, marching in line.

As it turned out I was never successful in my ant-swimming school, but, decades later, under my BSc in Biological Sciences, I discovered that many ants are incapable of swimming for various reasons—mainly when a peg crushes their heads.

In the end, I've learned a lesson from those poor ants. Suffering is an inescapable reality. Sometimes the world causes it. Sometimes we cause it. But most of the time—somebody else causes it. And all those times God is allowing it.

People often feel like those ants in the presence of a god who is the cosmic version of little me but if we look at the natural world, and if we look to the Scriptures, we'll see that, independently of the level of suffering we all experience in our lives, there is immense hope and profit in our pain.

C. S. Lewis once said this with authority in his book *The Problem of Pain*:

> God whispers in our ears in our pleasures, speaks through our conscience but screams through our pain, which is his megaphone to wake up a deafened world.[32]

But as it happens with all those who write about the subject, it's easier said than done. Decades later, after the death of his wife Joy, the grieving Lewis writes another book, *A Grief Observed*, and asks:

> What do people want to say when they affirm: "I am not afraid of God because I know how good he is?" Have they ever been to the dentist? (. . .) It doesn't matter whether you cling to the chair or leave your hands on your lap. The drill keeps on drilling.[33]

As all Christians do, I have approached the subject of suffering in my own life, as in the lives of others, from my perspective, since I believe it's futile to compare our sufferings. My pain might not be painful at all for somebody else and vice versa.

But we all suffer. And not only us, but suffering is apparently part of the fabric of biology. From ants that are crushed by an innocent child to wasps laying eggs inside caterpillars to the relationship between predator and prey. That fact remained even in the mind of the great biologist Charles Darwin, the man responsible for the framework of the theory of evolution we have today:

> That there is much suffering in the world no one disputes. Some have attempted to explain this in reference to man by imagining that it serves for his moral improvement. But the number of men in the world is as nothing compared with that of all other

sentient beings, and these often suffer greatly without any moral improvement. A being so powerful and so full of knowledge as a God who could create the Universe, is to our finite minds omnipotent and omniscient, and it revolts our understanding to suppose that his benevolence is not unbounded, for what advantage can there be in the sufferings of millions of the lower animals throughout almost endless time?[34]

I have wrestled with the same problem as well as Darwin's theory of evolution for a long time. But, although I am not anywhere near solving the first problem—that of the meaning of suffering—I've come to terms with the theory of evolution, and I now accept it as a traditional, solid Christian faith-compatible explanation for biological variety.[35]

Moreover, by blending those two problems together we might get some valuable insights for our own experiences. After all, God has used evolution and the suffering it produces to create the variety of life and complexity we have today. As I am about to explain, that does not, in any way, hamper my Christian view of reality—on the contrary, I believe that our vision of reality is greatly enriched as we can learn to see the suffering we all experience, or will experience, in the same way the apostle James learned.

Figure 10: "The Struggle for Existence" by George Bouverie Goddard, 1879. In his painting Goddard captures the whole idea of Darwin's theory. In the struggle for existence, only the fittest will survive and have better chances of reproduction. In the case of wolves, the alpha male that wins fights like that earns the right to reproduce with all females in the pack, and so its characteristics and variation (as Darwin puts it) will pass down to the descendants, improving chances of survival. But in the process, much suffering and pain takes place.

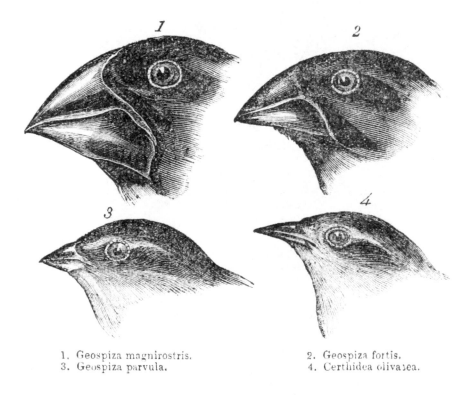

1. Geospiza magnirostris. 2. Geospiza fortis.
3. Geospiza parvula. 4. Certhidea olivasea.

**Figure 11: John Gould's depiction of Darwin's finches (before 1882).
Notice the variation due to the diet the birds were exposed to.**

Suffering is a fact of life on earth

Life on our planet is diverse and beautiful, but often we forget how fragile it is and how painful the existence of every living thing that lives on this planet is. That is the reality which staggers every biology undergraduate entering a laboratory to observe living things in the constant struggle for life and the "survival of the favoured species", as Charles Darwin called it.[36]

Indeed, suffering is the norm in our world, a truth we keep on forgetting, depending on the social situation we encounter. For example, the comfort of modern life allows us to eat hamburgers every day should we want to do so, but how many still remember that the burger is part of the muscle of a slaughtered animal?

Charles Darwin spent five years travelling around the world, meeting various types of biomes with different conditions of life. He collected data and samples, made sketches and descriptions of the most varied organisms; then, back in England, he spent twenty years studying and trying to understand how that variety of life came about—while his beloved daughter Anne slowly suffered from a chronic disease, which led to her early death after years of struggle.

How can one maintain faith in a God who allows for suffering to create beauty? Or, who allows for suffering to happen at all?

At the time, the general belief was that God had created all living things precisely as we see them today; but Darwin couldn't stop thinking of the small variations in the shaping of the beak of certain birds, the different body shapes of tortoises, iguanas, pigeons and other organisms that he observed.

He concluded that those tiny variations were the product of the differences in the environment where those animals lived. Those who were born with small variations could have an advantage when searching for food; therefore, they could survive. Over time, if no unpredictable event happened, the small differences would pile up inside the bodies, giving birth to new variations of that organism—or even, perhaps, if there was enough time, an organism completely different: a new species.

So, the exuberant biodiversity we see around us today (which is, unfortunately, decreasing every day), rich in colours, behaviour and mysteries, is the result of many individuals, incapable of adapting to a particular environment, going through pain and death. Every species of a living thing, including us humans, has been undergoing those modifications over time. That is what we call "evolution".

Since the idea of evolution is overloaded with emotion, people tend to say the concept is not compatible with the Bible. Especially when the logical conclusion is that God uses a lot of suffering and pain, including death, as the process by which he considers his creation "very good". But this line of thought precisely forgets the way Jesus lived his life as part of God's plan for our salvation:

> He was oppressed, and he was afflicted,
> yet he opened not his mouth;
> like a lamb that is led to the slaughter,
> and like a sheep that before its shearers is silent,
> so he opened not his mouth.
> By oppression and judgment he was taken away;
> and as for his generation, who considered
> that he was cut off out of the land of the living,
> stricken for the transgression of my people?
> And they made his grave with the wicked
> and with a rich man in his death,
> although he had done no violence,
> and there was no deceit in his mouth.
> Yet it was the will of the Lord to crush him;
> he has put him to grief;
> when his soul makes an offering for guilt,
> he shall see his offspring; he shall prolong his days;
> the will of the Lord shall prosper in his hand.
>
> *Isaiah 53:7–10*

Can you see that our salvation was an excruciating process for God? And that Jesus' death means our life? "Precious in the sight of the Lord is the death of his saints" (Psalm 116:15). God has always used pain, time, and death to perfect his creation—his sons, daughters, and his people. So why not his biodiversity? God the Father, Almighty, Maker of Heaven and Earth is the God of process, journey, and pilgrimage. To him, "one day is as a thousand years and a thousand years as one day" (2 Peter 3:8). "He who began a good work in you will bring it to completion at the day of Jesus Christ" (Philippians 1:6).

But isn't God's creation "very good"? How can suffering be "very good"? Referring to the last chapters of the Book of Job, Ronald E. Osborn comments:

> The God of the whirlwind — the God who takes responsibility for all of creation in all its strange, bewildering, endlessly innovative and untamed process—may leave us perplexed and dismayed. But lest we question the justice or goodness of God's ways in creating the eagle, the lion and the great sea monsters, we should ponder the verse that follows closely after the poem's vivid description of eagles feeding their young the blood of other animals. "Will the faultfinder contend with the Almighty?" God demands of Job (Job 40:2 NASB). It is a question we must continue to ask ourselves today.[37]

So, yes, suffering is very good. William Cowper, the great hymnwriter who suffered a lifelong struggle with depression, reaches the same conclusion:

> God moves in a mysterious way,
> His wonders to perform;
> He plants his footsteps in the sea,
> And rides upon the storm.
>
> . . .
>
> Judge not the Lord by feeble sense,
> But trust him for his grace;
> Behind a frowning providence,
> He hides a smiling face.[38]

In unison, the apostle James and many other biblical authors, along with our Lord Jesus, warn us that we will go through many trials in life but instead of looking at those trials or adversities as excuses to sin and lament, we can face everything trusting in God.

Suffering makes us resilient

Evolution is an idea applied to groups, not to individuals. You are not evolving now; no individual animal, plant, fungus, protozoan or bacterium is evolving. But their populations are, over a long period of time. All those life forms are competing against each other for survival, and humans are too. The successful life form (species) is the resilient one.

If a species wants to stay alive, to remain in existence, it must rapidly adapt to its environment to survive. It must have the correct adaptation for the right situation.

When I started my career as a science teacher, I kept flatworms, which are cute and measure 1 to 5 cm long, in a fish tank. They are fascinating to observe! (Figure 12) Even more impressive when you mutilate them into pieces.

When using a scalpel and slicing the animal into four separate parts, you don't kill it: instead, every single part regenerates into a new flatworm over the period of roughly a month. Such a trait is a good option of survival for the species in case the animal is crushed, stepped upon, cut, chewed (up to a point) or exposed to other events, such as a rendezvous with a science teacher; it is quite an experience to see the four parts moving independently. Talk about sheer will and skill of being alive!

Humans are a bit like flatworms in some ways, although we have very limited regeneration capacity, unlike them. But, apparently, they can "feel" pain, in a way like us. A study published in 2017 suggests that, like us, flatworms have a "dedicated system" for avoiding very hot or very cold environments.[39] They even respond to tissue damage, such as the one I used to inflict on them:

> Our results argue that the common ancestor of all bilateral animals probably had a cellular system to detect noxious stimuli . . . , one that worked using principles that are now broadly conserved in all animal groups. This scale of conservation is amazing, and we want to understand what else is conserved, and whether—like humans and flies—planarians may also possess a dedicated system for navigating innocuous hot and cold temperature.[40]

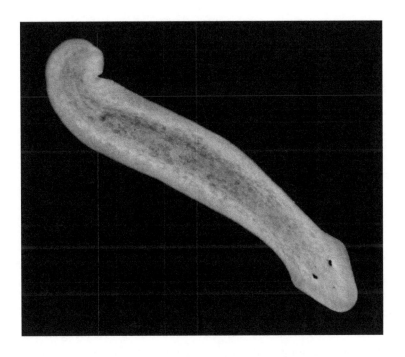

Figure 12: A species of flatworm (Platyhelminthes) called *Dugesia subtentaculatta*, not very different from the ones I used to experiment on in my first teaching year. Notice the two ocelli (not eyes) on the head, which are able to detect presence of light.

What that means is that the mechanism of feeling pain is so efficient and profitable to life that it is shared by all organisms that share a common ancestor with the flatworm, including humans. However, people would like to feel no pain at all, although the fact is that pain is one of our most essential mechanisms of self-protection, as the biologist Denis Alexander reminds us:

> . . . though we may not like the idea, pain is actually essential to our health and well-being. Pain is an essential property of animal life . . . Pain for us—as for all living organisms—is essential for survival.
>
> . . . Without pain we would be walking around on broken legs, happily going to school with meningitis, merrily ignoring fatal tumours and munching on broken glass with rotting teeth. In short, our lives would be considerably briefer than they are at present. So, pain is a practical good, which of course does not mean that we should not try to alleviate the suffering it brings, both in humans and in animals.[41]

Of course, valid as our biological description of pain might be, to feel pain is something completely different, so much so that we desperately try to avoid it. Cheap preaching even attracts people to churches on those empty promises, that God will simply "sort everything out". But, actually, Christian life won't always offer you freedom from pain, although it will still provide comfort and perspective, a way of seeing life, especially through the eyes of the apostle Paul, a man who experienced pain in various ways:

> For this light momentary affliction is preparing for us an eternal weight of glory beyond all comparison . . .
>
> *2 Corinthians 4:17*

> For as we share abundantly in Christ's sufferings, so through Christ we share abundantly in comfort too.
>
> *2 Corinthians 1:5*

Not only that, but we rejoice in our sufferings, knowing that
suffering produces endurance, and endurance produces character,
and character produces hope, and hope does not put us to shame,
because God's love has been poured into our hearts through the
Holy Spirit who has been given to us.

Romans 5:3–5

Not that I am speaking of being in need, for I have learned in
whatever situation I am to be content. I know how to be brought
low, and I know how to abound. In any and every circumstance,
I have learned the secret of facing plenty and hunger, abundance
and need. I can do all things through him who strengthens me.

Philippians 4:11–13

Suffering makes us more complex

The one who sees the evolution of living things as a journey towards
perfection is utterly mistaken. There is but a trend to increase the
complexity of living things. For example, animals with primitive eyes,
such as the flatworms we mentioned above, can only detect the presence
or absence of light, and survive the best they can in an on/off world.

Yet, God's creation is described as "very good".

Other animals, such as the famous *Biston betullaria*, or Mancunian
peppered moth (Figure 13), and my beloved ants, have hundreds of
smaller eyes that allow them to identify other environmental factors.

Because God's creation is "very good".

According to the theory of evolution, modifications like that came
about throughout the ages in response to increased exposure to sunlight,
with animals slowly but surely migrating from the bottom of the ocean
towards the surface, where light is abundant.

In that small paragraph you have just read, there are implicitly millions
upon millions of individuals who suffered and died, blind, hunted,
starving.

Does that make God's creation not "very good" then?

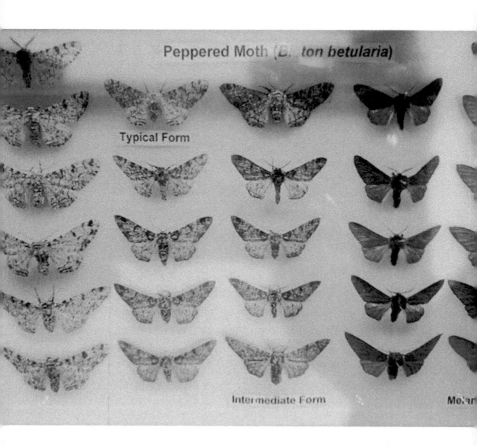

Peppered Moth (B. ton betularia)

Typical Form

Intermediate Form

Me;ar

Figure 13: Variations of *Biston betullaria*. Many variations of the animal can be seen in this picture taken by me in the Manchester Museum.

Figure 14: Christ healing the blind, Nicolas Colombel (1682).

We humans have only two very intricate eyes that can see but a fraction of the electromagnetic spectrum; even so, that doesn't mean we haven't evolved enough or we're not that perfect. Our eyes work very well, thank you very much. With them, we manage to see things around us; we manage to write, detect and produce beauty and read, particularly the Bible, where it is stated that God named his creation "very good".

Talking about the complexity of our eyes makes us remember the story of the man who was blind from birth, in John 9. His suffering made such an impression on Jesus' disciples that they could only explain the blind man's blindness in terms of a punishment for sin, whether his or that of his parents. They reduced the man, made in the image of God (albeit with a health condition), to a cosmic punishment.

But Jesus said: "It was not that this man sinned, or his parents, but that the works of God might be displayed in him." Jesus elevated the blind man to an instrument of God's glory, making his pain and story into life-transforming lessons for billions of people throughout history— but especially for the man himself, who to that point was nothing but a homeless blind man. John tells us the man was healed and, from a blind beggar, turned into an apologist in favour of Jesus, annoying and confusing the scholars and religious leaders of the area.

The man's suffering increased his complexity as a human being and as a person of faith. So much so that people, including his parents, were dazzled at his transformation. He "evolved", in a way. He was now more complete and had better vision than most, simply because he had had an experience with the Creator God. In James' words, he was now "perfect and complete, lacking in nothing".

Perseverance in the struggle for life

Those who argue that God could not have used evolution as a creative process, since it requires suffering and death, forget that pain (including death) is the tool that God continually uses in the lives of every single one of us, to make us more complete and complex Christians. To bring us closer to the image of Jesus Christ, our Lord. That is eschatological, for Ronald Osborn:

The creation was never a static golden age but always an unfolding story with an eschatological horizon. And the divine love has always willed that the journey of creation and pilgrimage of humanity should end in our final adoption as coheirs in God's kingdom and "partakers of the divine nature." The destiny of humankind is not simply a recapitulation or recurrence, paradise lost, paradise restored. Rather, the end is greater than the beginning—and was always meant to be through the mystery of incarnation.[42]

The Bible offers no resistance to evolution, when we read it with mind and heart open, and in light of the historical meaning of Genesis (see Chapter 5). The evolutionary process in the natural history of living things causes us to look inwards: our personal evolution, our change through time, towards Christlike Christians, demands that we experience suffering, as he did, but we can be grateful to God for those experiences, because they will bring an "eternal weight of glory beyond all comparison".

God is the creator of processes by his own choice. That process includes pain and suffering for all of us, including his own Son (one of us), the Holy Spirit and Himself, but don't be mad at God because of it. "Count it all joy, my brothers, when you meet trials of various kinds, for you know that the testing of your faith produces steadfastness. And let steadfastness have its full effect, that you may be perfect and complete, lacking in nothing." James says it all.

In your suffering, although it might be unbearable, do not rebel against God. C. S. Lewis warns us, he who had a go at trying to explain suffering but then experienced his share of it—like all the rest of us:

> Suppose you are up against a surgeon whose intentions are wholly good. The kinder and more conscientious he is, the more inexorably he will go on cutting. If he yielded to your entreaties, if he stopped before the operation was complete, all the pain up to that point would have been useless.[43]

When the surgery ends, though, you will have changed your evolutionary path. You will be a new, evolved Christian—"perfect and complete, lacking in nothing".

CHAPTER 4

Are we alone in the Universe?

When I look at your heavens, the work of your fingers,
the moon and the stars, which you have set in place,
what is man that you are mindful of him,
and the son of man that you care for him?
Yet you have made him a little lower than the heavenly beings
and crowned him with glory and honour.
You have given him dominion over the works of your hands;
you have put all things under his feet,
all sheep and oxen,
and also the beasts of the field,
the birds of the heavens, and the fish of the sea,
whatever passes along the paths of the seas.
O Lord, our Lord,
how majestic is your name in all the earth!

Psalm 8:3–9

Imagine you are dialling your radio when, suddenly, you find a frequency where you can only hear static. You are about to dial again, but you're distracted by someone calling your name. It's just your dad. Static continues sounding through the speakers. After a short exchange of words with dad, your hand is ready to turn the dial, but before you can do it, you hear two loud notes. You flinch. Static again. After two seconds, three notes. You find it weird but carry on listening. Two seconds later, five notes. Two seconds, seven notes. Now you know what to expect every two seconds. Eleven, thirteen, seventeen . . . and then all prime numbers up to 101. So, after ten seconds of static, the signal resumes as before—the same pattern.

Baffled, you wait for one more minute, thinking that static cannot produce a prime number sequence up to 101, in regular intervals. You are tempted to turn it off. But the signal keeps on repeating itself, as if teasing you. What would you do?

In the book (and film) *Contact*, by Carl Sagan, radio astronomer Ellie Arroway detects the same message.[44] She decides to record it and discovers a hidden instruction to build a machine and go to outer space. It turns out that it is the ultimate scientific discovery in history, which finally proves that humans are not alone in the Universe. Moreover, the aliens had written a set of instructions for the construction of the machine, capable of using Einstein-Rosen bridges—the famous "wormholes"—to travel over to the source of the signal, to the intelligence beyond planet Earth.

It would be incredible, were it not fiction.

Life on other planets has always been a fascination for humankind. The theologian and astrophysicist David Wilkinson traces back the origin of this fascination to the days of Plato, in the fourth century BC. According to Plato:

> [the creator of the Universe] spread out souls in equal number
> to the stars, inserting them in each one.[45]

But the search transformed from speculation to solid science in the twentieth century, especially with the SETI programme ("Search for Extra-terrestrial Intelligence"). It started as a small project in the 1960s, got funding of 100 million dollars in 1992, was closed by the American Congress in 1993 and has been operating as a non-profit research organization (as SETI Institute) as well as a scientific practice ever since.[46]

In the project radio telescopes (giant, robust satellite dishes, see Figure 15) are pointed up to different areas of the sky, collecting electromagnetic waves (such as radio waves) all the time. The amount of data is so vast that, to help with processing, SETI developed a software called SETI@Home, free to download and use. It keeps running in the background of one's computer, processing vast amounts of data sent over by the research projects. Until 2020, when the program was put in hibernation, more than 5 million volunteers had signed up and downloaded it.[47]

Even so, we still have only silence. Nobody has sent a signal from space, no ET has phoned home, and we have never listened to the final match of the Intergalactic Football League. However, scientists do not give up; the search for extra-terrestrial life, especially intelligent life, goes on, capturing the imagination of multitudes. Science fiction author Arthur C. Clarke phrased it well:

> There are two possibilities: either we are alone in the Universe, or we are not. Both are equally frightening.[48]

Why, though? Why is it frightening to be alone? That is a question to which science has not been able to provide an appropriate answer so far, and many doubt that it actually could, given its limitations, even though science can explain that:

> human beings are fundamentally and amply motivated by the need for belonging, i.e., for an intense desire of forming and keeping long-lasting interpersonal relationships. People often seek for positive interactions in a context of long-lasting, caring relationships.[49]

The need for belonging to a community of beings like us—metalheads, fans of a football team, supporters of the same political party, or intelligent beings capable of sending robots to other planets—is not absent from the Bible. The Church is precisely that—a community. But the author of Psalm 8 offers a perspective frequently underrated in our scientific age. Looking to the sky, one thinks about the magnitude of the Universe and comes back to the supposed insignificance of the human being, asking four deceptively simple questions. What is up there? Who is up there? Who is down here? What is down here?

Figure 15: Some radio telescopes of the Very Large Array (VLA), Socorro, New Mexico, USA. A set of twenty-eight spinning parabolic antennae of 25 metres across each, constantly capturing signals from outer space for hundreds of different scientific projects. Its construction spanned five years, from 1975 to 1980.

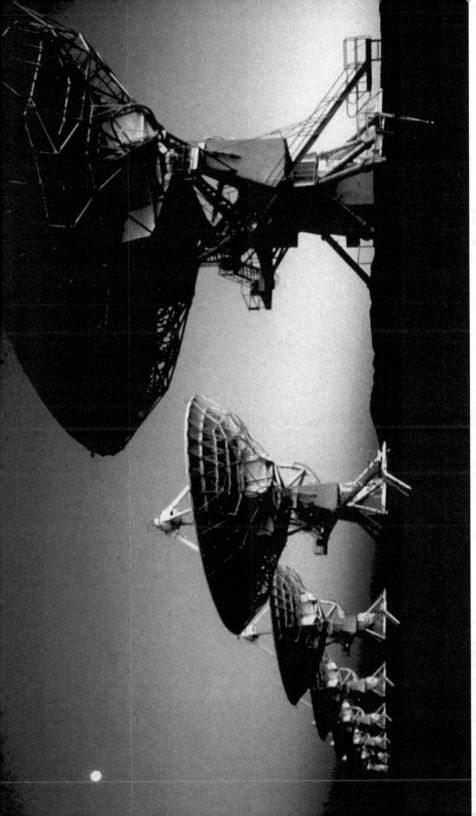

What is up there?

It is crucial to have a little context when reading the poem in Psalm 8. We read the words of a man who lived a long time ago, more than 2,000 years ago. We are not sure exactly when but certainly before the space race, modern science, Galileo, Copernicus, Ptolemy, and Aristotle. The world, then, was utterly different. There were no cars, no internet, no antibiotics, no science. Perhaps an excellent introduction to that Psalm would be: "a long time ago, in a galaxy far, far away . . . "

The ancients saw powerful gods in the celestial bodies. The Egyptians would see there the goddess Nut, bowing over the Earth with the stars embellishing her body. To the Mesopotamians, "astral bodies were the functional manifestations of divinity". The god of gods in the Babylonian pantheon, Marduk, the Sun-god, would have had the constellations engraved on the lower layer of the sky, made of jasper and thus determined the yearly calendar.[50]

The psalmists were possibly familiar with some of the myths of their time, like the ones mentioned. However, when looking up, they wouldn't see gods, nor would they see by-products of a sun-god. Rather, they would pay attention to the objects God had put up there for a reason.

Travelling back to the future into our twenty-first century, we point telescopes up and capture beautiful images, such as the one astronaut William Anders shot on Christmas Eve, 1968, while orbiting the moon on the lunar module of Apollo 8. The photo, shot from 250 million kilometres away, definitely does not show a god, but it shows our planet against a pitch-black background (Figure 17).

Less than a year later, humanity gave its first giant leap in space exploration, by landing on the moon. But the distances that were imperceptible to the Psalmist continue to be incomprehensible to us.

For example, the space probe New Horizons, launched in 2006, took nine years to reach Pluto. The probes Voyager 1 and 2, launched in 1977, left

Figure 16: Nut, the Egyptian goddess of the sky, depicted on the tomb of Ramses VI. She is swallowing up the sun, which will travel inside her body through the night and respawns in the morning.

Figure 17: Earthrise. The horizon is 780 km away from the
lunar module, where William Anders took the picture which,
according to photographer Galen Rowell, is "the most influential
environmental photograph ever taken". For the first time,
humanity realized (or felt) it was part of a vast universe.

Figure 18: Hubble Ultra-Deep Field. NASA/ESA. (2018) Almost
every point of light in this picture is a galaxy containing billions of
stars. The distance from us is about 13 billion light-years, i.e. less
than a billion years after the Big Bang—the origin of the Universe.
There are approximately ten thousand galaxies in that image.

the solar system in 2019, after forty-two years travelling faster than 55,000 km/h. However, they would need 70,000 years more to reach Proxima Centauri, the nearest star to the sun—provided no accidents happen.

But what about other galaxies, like Andromeda, the nearest one to us?

Virtually, they are impossible to reach in any predictable future. Our only hope is to use telescopes to study them, such as the world-famous Hubble Space Telescope, named after astronomer Edwin Hubble, whose discoveries allowed us to be sure that the Universe goes beyond our galaxy.

Launched in 1990, by NASA with the cooperation of the ESA (European Space Agency), the Hubble is a telescope orbiting our planet Earth, safe from ground vibrations and atmospheric interferences. Thus, it can shoot breath-taking photos of the farthest corners of the Universe. The images are taken daily and inspire scientists and artists alike.

From the thousands of images obtained, one became famous for a series of factors (Figure 18). Interestingly, it can provide a similar experience to the reading of Psalm 8. On both media, we see things from the past. In Psalm 8, we are told how people of past generations thought when stargazing, whereas in stargazing at Hubble Ultra-Deep Field, as it came to be known, we see what the stars looked like in the past, since light takes time to reach our eyes.

Light takes eight minutes to reach us from the sun, so what we see now reflects how it was eight minutes ago, not now. The further away a star is, the longer it takes for its light to reach us. By doing various calculations, scientists can determine the distance of a star or galaxy. Some galaxies in Figure 18 are more than 13 billion light-years away from us. That means the light has left that star 13 billion years ago—only a "few" million years after the Big Bang—and only reached Hubble's lenses in 2003. Looking to the image, we see galaxies that formed at the beginning of the Universe. All concentrated in a dark dot in the sky, smaller than a grain of sand, in the constellation of Fornax.

Every day astronomy discovers something. As you read this book, be confident it is already not up to date. We know of dozens of Earth-like planets throughout the Universe that may be able even to support life as we know it. Many people hope some of those may also harbour intelligent life. What will the next ten years of astronomical research show, we wonder?

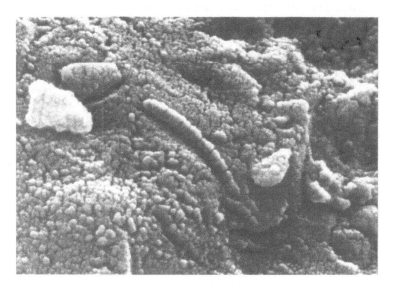

Figure 19: The rock ALH84001 (top) and a photograph of
the microscopic structures seen in it. Many believe that the
structures closely resemble earthbound bacteria, which led to
the hypothesis of contamination: perhaps Martian microbes (if
they exist) came to Earth. Or would it be the other way around?

So, what is up there after all? Not gods, but undoubtedly celestial bodies. Planets, stars, galaxies, quasars, pulsars, black holes, and all sorts of wonders that the Psalmist calls "the work of God's fingers". The image we gather from those words is of an artist sculpting his masterpiece:

> God Creator is the Artist
> He created our life.
> May there be others up there, writing Psalms?

Who is up there?

The Psalmist says that God made humankind "lower than the celestial beings". What "beings" does he have in mind? Was the Psalmist speaking of little green men? Is there evidence of life out there?

In 1996, a rock weighing around two kilogrammes, found in Antarctica twelve years before, became headline news after travelling around the solar system for more than 13,000 years. One NASA team, led by David McKay, reported they had found on that rock (named ALH84001) fossil evidence of microorganisms. One detail though: based on the composition of gas bubbles trapped in the rock, it was safe to say the rock had come from Mars. It would be the first evidence of extra-terrestrial life—were it not so controversial. Many scientists were not convinced. In 2021, the scientific community is still unsure about what to think when talking about ALH84001. Does it show fossils? Does it show structures like bacteria, but nothing more than that?

Whatever may be the case, the search for life outside our planet is an obsession of our age. How would it be any different? After the Apollo missions conquered the moon, proving it to be possible to land on other worlds and come back safely home, the Universe may be, in a way, more accessible to human beings. Who knows whether our dreams of finding others like us will be fulfilled?

So we started sending probes to space. The Voyagers, mentioned before, take with them wherever they go a golden record with information and recordings from Earth—including our location in the Universe, to make it easier if they want to come for tea—or maybe for doomsday!

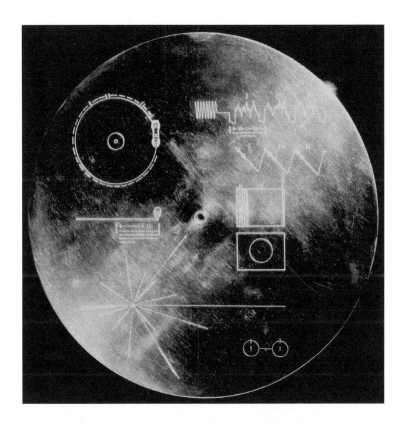

Figure 20: The Sounds of Earth, a golden disk attached to the
probes Voyager 1 and 2. It contains data about life on Earth and
especially humans in case the probe is intercepted by an alien race.

It is our nature to explore. We have sent more than a hundred successful missions to virtually all planets in the solar system. Between 1969 and 1972, twelve people walked on the surface of the moon (some even stumbled up there or drove vehicles around). In September 2020, NASA published its plans for the programme Artemis, where it states its plan for "landing humans on the Moon in 2024" and extending "lunar missions and preparing for Mars".[51]

But our neighbourhood is not enough. Another space telescope, Kepler, was launched to discover planets outside the solar system (called exoplanets), and scientists use other methods of detection in the observatories spread around the world. Every piece of news of the discovery of a new Earth-like planet leads people to ask: "Will it be this one?" It seems that the discovery of life on other worlds is only a matter of time—although many scientists are not that enthusiastic about it, like David Hughes, for example:

> First you have to point your radio telescope in the direction of a star that might be the parent of a planetary system . . . Then for each star you have to search a radio window that stretches from 1 to 10 GHz and contains 100,000 million 0.1 Hz bandwidth channels. No wonder you are thankful for your computer's Fourier transform superprocessor; no wonder you are worried about the fluctuations in the background noise resembling an artificial signal. And even overlooking the fact that your search might last for the lifetimes of many generations of scientists, you still have to contend with the fickle nature of scientific funding agencies who are only too happy at times to suggest that you are wasting your time and their money![52]

Will the scientific effort be in vain? Should the Church oppose such an inconsequential expenditure of money in a dull search in a haystack? To the theologian Theodore M. Hesburgh—of course not:

> It is precisely because I believe (theologically) in the existence of an infinite being called God, and that He is infinite in intelligence, freedom and power that I cannot, with a clear mind, take upon

myself limiting what He has created. Since he created the Big
Bang ... He could have foreseen the billions of directions to
which the Universe could evolve, including the billions of
different types of galaxies and various types of intelligent beings
... As a theologian, I would say that the proposal of the search
for extraterrestrial intelligence (SETI) is also a search for knowing
and understanding more of God through his works, especially the
ones who reveal him better. Finding others like us would mean
knowing God better.[53]

Based on our faith, as Christians we are not afraid of anything we might
find, as the Psalmist remembers. Wherever the search for extraterrestrial
life might take us, one thing will remain clear: whoever is up there (if)
is not an evolved being who comes to kidnap humans, as suggested by
the abduction stories—as true as they might be for the experiencers.
Whoever is up there (if) is not a god or gods in technological chariots.
But the One up there, beyond the realm of existence of any kind of life,
is the One who created the stars, heavens and celestial bodies which
capture our eyesight in a clear night, as well as any life form that could
inhabit those places.

And he is not alone. The Bible tells us of the identity of the "celestial
beings". Those are called "angels", serving God continuously. Those are
the "celestial beings" the Psalmist is talking about. God created them
for himself, but also to help us in our needs, as yet another Psalmist
reminds us:

> If you say, "The Lord is my refuge,"
>> and you make the Most High your dwelling,
>> no harm will overtake you,
>> no disaster will come near your tent.
> For he will command his angels concerning you
>> to guard you in all your ways;
>> they will lift you up in their hands,
>> so that you will not strike your foot against a stone.
>
> *Psalm 91:9–12 (NIV)*

The picture so far is this one: outside our atmosphere there are uncountable stars, planets, and possible life forms. There are powerful angels that serve God day and night. On Earth, we find a rich biodiversity, with millions of different life forms and marvellous landscapes.

What is it that makes us, humans, special—if indeed we are anything like that?

Who is down here?

The natural consequence of looking up is looking down, or rather, looking inside. The Psalmist does precisely that:

> When I look at your heavens, the work of your fingers,
> the moon and the stars, which you have set in place,
> what is man that you are mindful of him,
> and the son of man that you care for him?
>
> *Psalm 8:3–4*

Thousands of years later, in 1670, the scientist, mathematician and philosopher Blaise Pascal did exactly the same thing:

> When I consider the short duration of my life, swallowed up in the eternity before and after, the little space which I fill, and even can see, engulfed in the infinite immensity of spaces of which I am ignorant, and which know me not, I am frightened, and am astonished at being here rather than there ... Who has put me here? By whose order and direction have this place and time been allotted to me? ... The eternal silence of those infinite spaces frightens me.[54]

Apparently, there are people with a certain bias for presenting humanity, or planet Earth, as insignificant things in the Universe. That is especially true for the twentieth and twenty-first centuries. John Gribbin, in his book *Alone in the Universe* (note the title!), says:

> Since the time of Copernicus, the progress of science has resulted
> in a steady displacement of the perceived place of human beings
> from centre stage in the Universe. By the end of the twentieth
> century the received wisdom was that we are an ordinary kind
> of animal living on an ordinary planet orbiting an ordinary star
> in the backwoods of an unspectacular galaxy. But this image of
> the Earth and humankind as an insignificant unit in the Universe
> may be wrong.[55]

So, what is humanity compared to the infinity of the Universe around?

Well, the human being, *Homo sapiens sapiens*, is a vertebrate, a
mammal of the order of the primates, made up of trillions of eukaryotic
cells (with a nucleus containing its DNA), of about 200 different types,
organized in tissues, organs and systems. It is also a carbon-based life
form, as is every other life form known. Carbon is an element that forms
at very high temperatures (100 million degrees Celsius), in stars with half
the mass of the sun which exploded billions of years ago.

Such a life form inhabits a planet in the "habitable zone", the goldilocks
area of the solar system, around its star—a shorter or longer orbit would
mean a dead world, either by being too hot or too cold. But it is "just
right". Therefore, it contains around 70 per cent water in the liquid state
on the surface, and its axis is inclined 23.5 degrees, which allows for
well-defined weather systems and seasons.

Earth also has a solid, metallic core, which generates a magnetic field
around it, allowing that solar winds and explosions of dangerous particles
to living things are deflected to the poles, where almost no life exists. Our
planet also has a thin atmosphere, whose gas concentration generates
a gentle greenhouse effect, keeping the temperature in delightful
boundaries.

Moreover, 4.5 billion years ago, Earth was hit by a huge rocky body
and later, 65 million years ago, by another one, much smaller. Collisions
such as these produced the moon, responsible for the tidal movements,
the tilted axis of the planet, and the extinction of dinosaurs, clearing the
way for the mammal dominance and consequently, for the evolution of
humans.

However, the human being is much more than its biology or natural history. Humans are self-conscious beings, capable of asking questions about themselves, the past, present and future and the meaning of the Universe. Or rather, the reason behind the Universe. Humans live with the feet on the ground and the mind in the stars and beyond. It is the only living thing known so far that builds mass destruction weaponry besides writing love letters or poems.

Human beings think about death and desperately try to avoid it. Thus, they invented medicine, discovered antibiotics and study their own bodies as well as others', to cure pain.

It is not good for human beings to be alone (Genesis 2:18), so they live searching for other humans that complete them, amuse them, to have communion with and to make them feel not alienated, not different, but part of a community, part of a family.

The Psalmist is not thinking about all that when talking about the human being, though. Remember, there was no science back then! Rather, he is possibly thinking of the Mesopotamians, who believed that humans were created to bear the load of the gods. But the God of Abraham, Isaac and Jacob would not do that. He created extraordinary beings "a little lower than the heavenly beings and crowned [them] with glory and honour" and made them his representatives to govern creation. God has not created images of himself, as other gods would have done. Instead, God created us as his image.

God created the human being with love and interest (Psalm 8:4), like a father who looks after his children—his family, who in turn take care of the planet he created. And, as any creator would, God has created a wonderful place for his children to live in.

What is down here?

One of the main objections to SETI is the spending of so much money in other planets' affairs when there is so much suffering on our planet. A lot of that suffering is the product of human action, including science and technology. After all, the current problem of plastic in the ocean would not exist without plastic—one of the most versatile materials ever invented.

Figure 21: Food chains and webs are complex energy flow diagrams that represent the interdependence between organisms. In the picture, a lioness is hunting a Cape Buffalo, which eats vegetation from the Serengeti National Park, which in its turn provides energy for many other animals. When the lioness dies, the energy stored in her body will return to the ecosystem, through decomposers.

Our planet is unique. The ecological relationships between living things are so intricate that the destruction of one ecosystem, such as the deforestation of the Amazon rainforest, promotes extinction to many living things and messes with weather systems.

The Psalmist knows what is down here, though: "the work of God's hands" (Psalm 8:6). He goes on saying that cattle, wild animals, birds and virtually all animals known and valued by the ancient civilizations, are under the dominion of human beings.

We ought to be careful with the word "dominion" because the image in Psalm 8 is not of a tyrant exploiting resources to his heart's content. Quite the contrary, humans are the governor or regent; they are the image of God, representatives that govern in his place, while he is "away" (not absent, but not seen). God wants the relationship with humans to develop with the many different life forms in the same way he relates to us: with care, love and respect, recalls Claus Westermann:

> The simple fact that the first page of the Bible speaks about heaven and earth, the Sun, the Moon, and stars, about plants and trees, about birds, fish, and animals, is a certain sign that the God whom we acknowledge in the Creed as the Father of Jesus Christ is concerned with all these creatures, and not merely with humans. A God who is understood only as the god of humankind is no longer the God of the Bible.[56]

Contact and communion

We have seen that humans probe the Universe in search of signals of other life forms, including intelligent life. The critical discovery of such beings would give us the certainty we are not alone in the Universe—at least, biologically speaking. Many people would feel maybe less solitary, less insignificant, reflecting what the aliens say in the film *Contact*:

> In our journey through existence, the only thing that makes the void bearable is each other.[57]

But independently of what the search for extraterrestrial life might show in the future, something is sure: God does not consider any of us insignificant, as Psalm 8 reminds us. Humans and the Universe are the creation of a merciful, loving God, who considers each human unique, that trusts him or her as his representatives who can care for creation, including the production of a science which they can understand, enhance and care for.

We return to Blaise Pascal, who asked the fundamental question of the Psalmist: "What are human beings, that God cares for them?" He offers a provocative answer in his book *Pensées*:

> If we say the man is too insignificant to deserve communion with God, we must indeed be very great to judge of it.[58]

The creator of the Universe and creatures proclaiming the work of his hand and his glory (Psalm 19) became part of his creation. There is still no evidence of intelligent extraterrestrials trying to communicate with us. But God became one of us, in the person of Jesus Christ—Emmanuel, the "God-with-us". Not so that he could study us, but that he could die in our place and restore our relationship with God in his resurrection. He reminds us, in John 14, that we will never be alone. In Matthew 28, he says he will be with us every single day. The best thing about that is, to contact him, one does not need either telescopes or doctorates—only an honest prayer.

Figure 22: "How the Ancient Hebrews Saw the World", Rachael Ayers, 2020, drawn for this book. The illustration aims to reflect how the ancient Hebrews that read Genesis might have understood the world. It was a disc supported by huge pillars. There was water, chaotic water, all around it, and a mighty multiple-headed serpent called Leviathan ruled it. The sky was the inner part of a solid dome, separating the waters. When it rained, it rained through windows opened in the dome. In the centre of the picture one sees the temple, the core of God's reign, who was above everything else, in Heaven.

CHAPTER 5

A new (old) way of reading Genesis 1

In the beginning, God created the heavens and the earth. The
earth was without form and void, and darkness was over the
face of the deep. And the Spirit of God was hovering over the
face of the waters.

And God said . . .

Genesis 1:1–3

Have you ever heard the proverb "whoever keeps staring at one tree,
misses the whole forest"? It is a Brazilian proverb, a variation of the
popular saying "being unable to see the wood for the trees". The idea in
the Brazilian version is that one keeps staring at one detail, thus missing
the lavishness and beauty of the whole picture.

Many people approach the tale of creation at the beginning of the Bible
precisely like that. They lock and load evidence of cosmic evolution or lack
thereof. Some make questionable assumptions (often utterly mistaken)
about the days of Genesis and the age of the Universe. Others try to use
the text to tell scientists that evolution or the "Big Bang" is impossible, or
that natural selection is biblical, contrary to macroevolution—and so on.

Many of us end up in that whirlwind of confusion, without realizing
that the anxiety of the modern (and post-modern) reader who approaches
Genesis all but disappears when one asks straightforward questions and
seeks the answers to them.

"When was that text written?"

More than two millennia ago. This simplicity hides a variety of facts,
though, which we will explore in this chapter.

Firstly, since it is ancient, the account was conceived, written and
edited well before any seed of modern science was sown. Whoever

authored Genesis, Moses (according to the tradition and many scholars) or other people (according to other scholars), never worried over the shape of the Earth, the Big Bang, natural selection, relativity or quantum physics. Those things simply did not exist in those days. In short, the text was written way before any science existed. From that point, a second question comes forth.

"Which questions does the text address?"

Surely there is nothing about dinosaurs, which is a word invented in the nineteenth century. There is nothing about the classification of living things into groups such as mammals, birds, amphibians, reptiles, etc. Such classification started with Aristotle (in Greece, far away from Israel, both in space and time) and picked up steam with the biologist Carl Linnaeus, in the eighteenth century CE. Genesis 1 does not seek to describe the sun as a star or the moon as a spherical satellite covered in regolith; neither does it mention the Earth's axis' inclination of 23.5 degrees.

Again, those concepts did not exist in antiquity. Figure 22 shows, based on the seven accounts of creation in the Bible,[59] the cosmology Israelites and many other peoples around them supported at the time they were reading Genesis for the first time. That was the accepted view of the Universe back then. Notice that the book is in the Old Testament, which is Scripture for Jews and Christians, so equally valid to all of them when they would talk about the origins of *their* Universe.

By the way, is the text also describing the origin of *our* Universe, or something else entirely? Perhaps the intention of the author is not to talk only about the material world we're in, but about the way a specific audience should understand *their* place in the Universe as *they* understood it. Which brings us to the third question.

"What is the lesson the text is trying to teach?"

From a scientific standpoint, one cannot say God has (or has not) created the Universe. Science is not concerned with questions of that type (see Chapter 2). Now, Christians might find the theme difficult because they believe in the authority of Scripture as the Word of God, infallible, inerrant and wholly profitable, although these words might mean different things for different traditions. To many of them, if atheistic arguments can falsify the Bible, or prove it wrong, then the Christian faith collapses since the entirety of its system of beliefs comes from the book. But you can let out a sigh of relief. No scientist can use Genesis when talking about science to make God useless or to falsify the Bible. Firstly, nobody would pay money for researching something that science does not worry about or has no instruments or tools to explore—such as God, who doesn't fit in boiling tubes or conical flasks. Secondly, Genesis 1 is not describing the Big Bang, evolution, relativity or science—at all.

Genesis 1 is not a scientific text (as we use the word nowadays). It is not about the creation of the Universe as we understand it in the twenty-first century. This Universe of big bangs, red-shifted galaxies, supernovas, evolution and DNA did not exist as an explanation back then, as we saw. Instead, according to John H. Walton, Genesis 1 is most likely about the inauguration of a Cosmic Temple.[60] That last sentence might be a new thought for many readers, so let it sink in for a moment.

Genesis 1 is telling the story of how God created his cosmic temple in six days, so he could enjoy it from the seventh day on in relationship with his creatures and his most valued representative: humankind.

We are going to explore those questions in some detail, so we can understand what is going on. Imagine you are travelling back in time, to a world of deserts, gods at war, stone tablets and scrolls.

When was Genesis 1 written?

Genesis was written at a time when gods were constantly at war. John Walton explains that peoples would measure their success or failure through divine action in their history:

> Deity pervaded the ancient world. Nothing happened independently of deity. The gods did not "intervene" because that would assume that there was a world of events outside of them that they could step into and out of. The Israelites, along with everyone else in the ancient world, believed instead that every event was the act of deity—that every plant that grew, every baby born, every drop of rain and every climatic disaster was an act

of God. No "natural" laws governed the cosmos; deity ran the
cosmos or was inherent in it. There were no "miracles" (in the
sense of events deviating from that which was "natural"), there
were only signs of the deity's activity (sometimes favourable,
sometimes not). The idea that deity got things running then
just stood back or engaged himself elsewhere (deism) would
have been laughable in the ancient world because it was not
even conceivable. As suggested by Richard Bube, if God were to
unplug himself in that way from the cosmos, we and everything
else in the cosmos would simply cease to exist. There is nothing
"natural" about the world in biblical theology, nor should there
be in ours. This does not suggest that God micromanages the
world, only that he is thoroughly involved in the operations and
functions of the world.[61]

For example, Egyptians saw in the world the deeds of many gods. The
periods of fertility in the Nile Valley had to do with divine will, as well
as light and darkness, rain, the terrible cloud of locusts—a force to be
reckoned with by the ancients—and the birth of Pharaoh's son. Even in
different areas of Egypt, the accounts of creation (henceforth, "myths")
would vary.

In Mesopotamia, the birthplace of one of the most famous creation
myths of the ancient world, the *Enuma Elish*, various gods, in cosmic
battles, create the world from the dismembered body of the goddess
Tiamat. Leading the enterprise is Marduk, the creator of the planets,
constellations, and the rivers Tigris and Euphrates:

> Marduk then declares his intention of establishing his own house
> in front of Essharra as his "cult centre", whereby the gods can find
> rest whenever they want. This is Babylon, the guest house of the
> gods and, thus, "the centre of religion".[62]

In that myth, humanity had been created by the goddess Mami, to "bear
the load of the gods", an idea not very different from what we want to do
with robots in our time!

Figure 23: Ptah, the Lord of Order, from a Memphis Egyptian creation myth: "He commands order in the cosmos for life and dominion. He, who made totality and caused the gods to evolve, is Ta-tenen, the land that becomes distinct."

Figure 24: An engraving plate from Mesopotamia, from around 1000 BCE, showing (probably) Tiamat (left) being attacked by Marduk with thunderbolts (right). From the Enuma Elish: "The moon he caused to shine, the night to him entrusting. He appointed him a creature of the night to signify the days: "Monthly, without cease, from designs with a crown. At the month's very start, rising over the land, You shall have luminous horns to signify six days, On the seventh day reaching a half-crown."

We cannot forget Canaan, and in it, there is a god extremely relevant for the Old Testament: Ba'al. In their creation myth, Ba'al battles Yamm, or the god of the sea, and the "twisting serpent", Litan, the sea monster. And he wins. After his victory and the offering of a banquet to the gods, he builds his residence, taking seven days to finish his construction.

The similarity of those myths with Genesis 1 is striking. Some people would argue, kind of hastily, that because of that similarity Genesis is not more than a cheap copy of those other myths. However, the differences between all the accounts and Genesis 1 are so profound one cannot seriously defend that position. In that way, Genesis is an answer to those other myths from the Israelite perspective.

To start with, there are no gods at war in Genesis 1. There is only one God. There is chaos, like in the other myths, represented by the waters. However, in Genesis the disorder is not regarded as bad. It is just there. In the beginning, God created heaven and earth, which was formless, unrecognizable, and *void*, without inhabitants. God, who is completely satisfied before the inauguration of the world, decides to create. He does not do it to defeat monsters; he does not mutilate other gods (because they don't exist) and certainly does not create to take it easy by overloading minor slaves called humans. Instead he focuses his attention on our world and will work on it for six days (which should be our working pattern too) building a temple for himself, where he is going to dwell, rest and enjoy his creation, which is "very good".

There is no fight for dominion. No games played by the powers that be. There is a block of stone and an artist expecting to start sculpting. Any Mesopotamian, Egyptian or Canaanite who stopped and talked with an Israelite foreigner would be surprised in knowing that the Israelite wouldn't understand himself as God's slave but as made in his *image*, a representative to the rest of the world, including the animals.

Think about it this way. The experience of immigrating is a profound one. Immigrants frequently start their new lives with no possessions, often house-sharing for a while, while making some money. They also receive a work permit and are registered to pay taxes whilst continuing to look for a place to live. Finally, after long days of hard work, they manage to find a place to call "home". From that moment on, the immigrants begin to fully reside in the new country—and enjoy life.

As we said before, according to an ancient tradition and indications of the Old Testament itself (for example, Deuteronomy 31:24), Genesis, as well as the other four first books of the Bible, a collection called "Pentateuch" or "Torah", was written by Moses, during and after the Exodus from Egypt. Alternatively, we can concede that the account was edited from a source tradition or contained "post-mosaic additions" by different people,[63] perhaps even during Ezra's time (fifth to sixth centuries BCE), during the return from Babylonian captivity, centuries after Israel's departure from Egypt. For our purposes, this does not matter. In both cases, we can understand that the text is speaking to immigrants facing the forces of chaos, immigration and pilgrimage. It is unlikely that any Israelite, in any of those situations, would spend time thinking about the origin or nature of those lights hanging from the solid, glass-like dome we call "sky" or how the beasts of chaos speciated, for the simple reason that it did not matter at all.

Think back on the urgency in the life of immigrants. When they secure their new house, they probably won't ask about the materials, the brand of paint used on the walls, the history of the architecture or the family tree of the owners etc. They just want a roof to sleep under.

Less dramatically, the person who buys a computer does not worry about the hardware specialist who built it, nor about the material that constitutes the wiring of the machine. Some people will worry about those things, but not most people. Most of the customers are not interested in how long it took for the technology of micro processing to arise when shopping for a gaming computer.

For all purposes, one might say the computer did not exist at all before being bought. It was not on my desk, so *it wasn't*. After buying it, though, it serves a function. Does it work? Good enough.

In the same way, the author of Genesis and its editors did not write or edit it for a minority of initiated ancient scholars. It was meant to communicate with immigrants either wandering in the *formless and void* desert between Egypt and Canaan for decades, or for months between Babylon and Jerusalem, which lies abandoned, miles away, *formless and void*. However, in either case, the reader addressed is a part of the chosen people of God, descendants of Abraham, heirs of that portion of land which is so precious and *holy* to them. In the case of the freed slaves from Egypt, it is the Promised Land promised by the God of Abraham, Isaac and Jacob, who sends them there to worship, to a place where the Tabernacle and the Ark of the Covenant can finally rest.

If the readers were Israelites coming back to Canaan after decades of Babylonian forced labour, they are a people whose temple had been destroyed. They had had no place to worship YHWH for two entire generations. And that is on them. The Temple's obliteration was due to the people's disobedience or, in other words, due to them doing that which God forbade them to do. Pretty much like Adam and Eve in the garden, they had known sin. But now, they are coming back to rebuild the Temple. And they will do it in such a way that the Sabbath must now be respected and the land tended, expelling chaos from it, like it was "in the beginning, [when] God created the heavens and the earth".

Genesis 1 communicates to those groups first, and it would have made complete sense to both in each specific situation. In the first case, people trying to find their religious and cultural identity; in the second case, people in search of a religious and cultural identity lost due to sin. Neither of the two groups would be interested in the material origin of the world, but they needed reminding of how God organized his creation from "*formless and void*" to "*very good*". Their very lives needed just that.

What questions is Genesis 1 trying to answer?

The desert is vast. Empty (void) except for the uncanny wild animals and strange critters living under the rocks. Occasionally a peculiar plant. Unbearably hot and bright during the day and unbearably cold and dark in the night. Why is that? Bear in mind that there is no science to help you answer that. You are thousands of years before a scientific explanation is offered.

Well, the desert is chaotic, nothing *exists* in it, as John Walton explains:

> I propose that people in the ancient world believed that something existed not by virtue of its material properties, but by virtue of its *having a function in an ordered system*. Here I do not refer to an ordered system in scientific terms, but an ordered system in

human terms, *that is, in relation to society and culture.* (emphasis
is ours)[64]

It might be hard to get your head around it, but we have a modern
example. When a child is born, his or her birth needs to be formally
registered and a birth certificate needs to be issued. Until that happens,
that child does not exist as a person with rights or obligations. He or she
does not exist, until their parents sort the problem out by registering it.
The same applies to schools, organizations, weddings. Until the proper
documentation is sorted, those things are only non-existent ideas.

According to Walton, a similar logic is present in Genesis 1. No
people exist in the desert, in the in-between land. Who can solve the
problem of travelling through the chaos of the desert? Why, God! His
Spirit hovers over it, and his voice transforms the *formless and void* into
things with form and function—giving them utility and existence, like
rocks springing much needed water, or dew turning into bread, or clouds
protecting from the sun and fire from the cold.

Very different people perceive the world in very different ways. As
modern readers studying Genesis and imagining God creating the world,
we need to forget that the world is kind of spherical, that it is suspended
in the solar system by gravity, in the Milky Way, in the Local Group. One
must ignore the periodic table, and everything science has come up with
to explain the world. One has even to forget that plants are organisms
and only think of them in terms of a food source. Forget bacteria and the
cell theory. In fact, forget biology, physics and chemistry. The Universe in
Genesis 1 was much simpler—and people were absolutely fine with that
back then. So why shouldn't we be, when visiting *their* world through
reading?

Try and imagine the world as they understood it. Figure 22 was
envisioned to help you with that. The earth disc is supported by
immense rocky pillars, with seas all around. Among the pillars, there
lies an enormous sea monster, the serpent, Leviathan, sidewinding in the
ocean. There was only one continent, where the human drama unfolds.
Above all, there was a solid dome of glass or crystal, from which stars,
sun and moon were hanging; there were some "windows" here and
there, through which rain would come. (There were no planets because

those were discovered and named by the Greeks, centuries later.) Over the dome there was more water and heavens would be above it, where one would find God's throne, and the divine council, where seraphim, cherubim and angels are—outside the world and everything that exists *for God and for us.*

How did our atoms come about? What made them become helium, carbon, gold? How did they organize in molecules of life? How did animals change over time from their common ancestors? Don't look for answers to those questions in Genesis because that book is not describing our understanding of the world's origin. It is describing the *Ancient Israelites'* understanding of the world's origin: the ancient world. Better still, Genesis 1 is telling *us,* people from all ages, how God organized the formless and void chaos, even though it was harmless to him, into a temple for himself. And it is written like that because it is communicating with people going through formless and void places, be it from the exile to the promised land, captivity to freedom, Syria to the UK, Europe to America, Africa to Brazil, infancy to adulthood, unemployment to career, slavery to freedom, sin to grace, in search of identity, through chaos, in need of order and God.

How then did God create the world? He is All-Mighty. He needs no help to do his bidding. So, he creates by commanding. He commands, and creation obeys. He does not do everything at once, but step by step, taking *his* time, analysing, and evaluating his work, enjoying the whole process in eight creative acts and ten commandments![65] He is indeed an artist! Worthy of a work-of-art such as the creation account in Genesis 1.

There is no millions-of-years, evolution, Big Bang, natural selection nor anything of the like in the text. We might understand that God, through his commands, kick-started all those processes, but that would be a modern application of the text, not its literal meaning.

Genesis 1 has been called a "creation manifesto", written to teach the Israelites, and other ancient people, that the whole Universe is the handiwork of a Person *forming* it through his words. Likewise, the *form* of the text is organized, symmetrical. On the first, second and third days, God assigns (creates) *functions* for light, sky (the dome) and waters, land and vegetation (food). Light now serves as a tool to organize night and day. The sky stays above all, holding the waters. A dry portion now exists for *somebody* to step on, and to support vegetation. It is not formless anymore, but it is still *void*. So, on days four, five and six, God creates *functionaries*, which give meaning to the functions which exist, which occupy the spaces. The sun, moon and stars occupy the dome, producing light or darkness according to their "seasons"; birds occupy the sky, the space between firmament (the glass-like dome) and land, and aquatic life occupies the sea; animals, crawlers and human beings occupy the land and eat vegetation.

Then, on day seven, God rests and enjoys his complete work, both existent and functioning. And everything is "very good" (Genesis 1:31). Space and time now unite in a worshipful existence. William Brown notes:

> The Universe, it turns out, is a cosmic temple in time. Its "entrance" is demarcated by Days 1 and 4, together with designating the creation of light and lights, respectively. Not coincidentally, the Solomonic Temple in Jerusalem faced eastward to welcome the rising sun.[66]

What does Genesis 1 want to teach?

The sixth day is the busiest in the creation, and it is on that day that God creates humankind—not the two people we call "Adam" and "Eve", you see. Genesis 1:26–27 (NIV) says:

> Then God said, "Let us make mankind in our image, in our likeness, so that they may rule over the fish in the sea and the birds in the sky, over the livestock and all the wild animals, and over all the creatures that move along the ground."

> So God created mankind in his own image,
> in the image of God he created them;
> male and female he created them.

The text in which human beings are created from the dust is in Genesis 2, a second creation account, with a completely different structure from Genesis 1, and it focuses on humankind. We are not interested in it in this book. But when God says, in Genesis 1:26, "let us create man . . .", the Hebrew word for "man" is *adam*, which is not translated (in any English translation) into the name Adam, in that portion of the Scripture. In verse 26, therefore, God creates humankind.

The humankind God creates is not a slave, nor is it a by-product of a cosmic battle. God creates man in his likeness, his image. Zachariah Zienka explains what that means:

> The opening chapters of Genesis shook the ancient world with a bold claim. All humans are made in the image of God. That was and still is revolutionary, but what does it mean to be made "in the image of God"? What is Genesis trying to convey? Why is this such a powerful idea? In the ancient world (specifically the Ancient Near East), to "be made in the image of a god" was a depiction reserved for only two things: idols and kings. When Genesis uses the phrase "image of God," it uses the Hebrew word "*tselem*" for "image." You might be surprised to learn this, but "*tselem*" is often translated as "idol" in our Bibles—"the idols of God".[67]

An idol represents the presence of the king or god among us. It's been said that, in the Ten Commandments, God forbids the manufacture and worship of idols for a straightforward reason: we, humans, are the images, idols, "*tselem*" that God has already made. So, as Zachariah Zienka argues, to build and worship an idol is to forfeit our own nature. We might add it is to have a degenerated self-esteem too.

The creation of humanity is the climax of Genesis 1. God has created a temple for himself—the Universe—and he organized everything for a "very good" (notice: not perfect) creation. But he would rest on the seventh day, as someone who would enjoy his recently built new office. One can picture the owner finally sitting down on the sofa and starting their work—as the president or prime minister after the hard work of campaigning finally sits down in the office to rule the country.

Alternatively, like González argues, it is as if God can now trust someone to take care of his work while he enjoys it:

> We often speak of the presence of God, and rightly so. But this other theme or metaphor of absence is also common in the Bible. Even apart from sin, God gives the human creature space, freedom to exercise its responsibility. . . . In the story of the garden, after creating humans and giving them dominion over the rest of creation, God lets them exercise that dominion, even though it also implies the possibility of sin. And this absence, just as much as the divine presence, is a sign of love.[68]

Thus, God created humankind as his representative. Still, on the theme of the temple, humanity is the only part of creation with a priestly responsibility. Humankind will have dominion over creation. But that doesn't mean *exploitation*. It means to rule. And the ruler *serves*, be that ruler Moses, Joshua, David, Ezra, Nehemiah, President, King, Prime Minister, politician, teacher, manager. Or indeed, Jesus. And the good ruler serves the subjects. Sure, the ruler also controls, so that chaos doesn't ever come back. But he does that with love, care and responsibility—and ultimately with sacrifice.

What should we do with the world created in Genesis 1?

Genesis 1 is not meant for us to discuss and decide between creation and evolution. It is not a text that reveals a secret code for people to figure out, as an initiation for a gnostic cult of the chosen ones.[69] Genesis is not a science textbook either. But it is a manifesto. In Genesis, we learn that all the chaos, formlessness and void in creation can and will be subdued and worked out by God, the creator. Creation is his biggest temple, and it is very good, so he would never abandon it. Moreover, we are his images, his representatives, his priests, who should be taking care of the temple while he is "resting". Justo González, again, reminds us of that:

> Ours is a God who rests, a God who is not always available . . .
> There is much Christian preaching that ignores this. We are told
> that if we want something, all we have to do is pray, and if we have
> enough faith God will give it to us. This denies and undercuts the
> sovereignty of God. God is not like a drink-dispensing machine:
> you put in your coins, and out comes the drink. Such a god is in
> truth an idol, a god constantly and continually at our disposal,
> ready to do our bidding.[70]

Like in the Parable of the Talents, in Matthew 25, to some God gave
a little responsibility, to others a bit more, and to some others, a lot of
responsibility for caring for the vineyard. One day he will come back.
He'll ask us to approach his throne and report back on what we have
been doing about it. What will we say? That we took care of his creation?
Or that, afraid of him, we let his garden be overrun by weeds and pests?

Or even worse: are we going to say that we burned his forests, killed
his wild animals, extinguished his birds and killed the marine life so that
we could live more comfortably? Are we going to say we took away the
identity of people by allowing them to become climate refugees so we
could have a comfortable lifestyle?

A biblical collage

The beginning

In the beginning God created the heavens and the earth. (. . .)
God saw all that he had made, and it was very good . . .

Genesis 1:1,31 (NIV)

So God created man in his own image,
in the image of God he created him;
male and female he created them.

Genesis 1:27

Now the Lord had planted a garden in the East, in Eden; and
there he put the man he had formed (. . .) The Lord took the man
and put him in the Garden of Eden to work it and take care of it.

Genesis 2:8,15 (NIV)

When the woman saw that the fruit of the tree was good for food
and pleasing to the eye, and also desirable for gaining wisdom,
she took some and ate it. She also gave some to her husband who
was with her, and he ate it.

Genesis 3:6 (NIV)

[God] said: Because you listened to your wife and ate the fruit
from the tree about which I commanded you, "You must not
eat from it,"

Cursed is the ground because of you;
through painful toil you will eat food from it all the days of your life.
It will produce thorns and thistles for you,

and you will eat the plants of the field.
By the sweat of your brow
you will eat your food
until you return to the ground,
since from it you were taken;
for dust you are
and to dust you will return

Genesis 3:17–19 (NIV)

Present day

... the creation waits in eager expectation for the children of God
to be revealed. For the creation was subject to frustration, not by
its own choice, but by the will of the one who subjected it, in hope
that the creation itself will be liberated from its bondage to decay
and brought into the freedom and glory of the children of God.

Romans 8:19–21 (NIV)

... if anyone is in Christ, the new creation has come: The old
has gone, the new is here! ... God was reconciling the world to
himself in Christ ...

2 Corinthians 5:17,19 (NIV)

The future

And the twenty-four elders, who were seated on their thrones
before God, fell on their faces and worshipped God, saying:

"We give thanks to you, Lord God Almighty,
the One who is and who was,
because you have taken your great power
and have begun to reign.
The nations were angry,
and your wrath has come.

The time has come for judging the dead,
and for rewarding your servants the prophets
and your people who revere your name,
both great and small —
and for destroying those who destroy the earth."

Revelation 11:16–18 (NIV)

A new beginning

Then the angel showed me the river of the water of life, as clear as crystal, flowing from the throne of God and of the Lamb down the middle of the great street of the city. On each side of the river stood the tree of life, bearing twelve crops of fruit, yielding its fruit every month. And the leaves of the tree are for the healing of the nations. No longer will there be any curse. The throne of God and of the Lamb will be in the city, and his servants will serve him. (...)

And they will reign for ever and ever.

Revelation 22:1–5 (NIV)

CHAPTER 6

The gardener who would be king

The world has changed. You know that. Twenty-five years ago, children were learning lessons about the rising of the sea level and entire coastal cities disappearing by the end of the twenty-first century. Listening to those things was, for many, complete science fiction. It imparted pretty much the same feeling as reading the book of Revelation the way many people read it: as a nightmarish hallucination about the end of the world.

How is it now, a quarter of a century later? Well, children are taking time out of school to go protesting, demanding change on things they don't fully understand, but know are bad news. One of them, Greta Thunberg, became world-famous after rising as an internationally acclaimed advocate against climate change at age fifteen, protesting against government inaction concerning climate change; she met world leaders, accusing politicians, among other things, of being reckless with the future of humankind and the planet, because of the faults and selfishness of older generations, which led to the climatic chaos seen worldwide.

Moreover, in 2019, the United Kingdom saw the rise of a movement called Extinction Rebellion, in which thousands of people, including children, took to the streets to protest against government inaction concerning mass extinction and social collapse.[71] To many ears, their message was ringing as one of fear about the upcoming unpredictable decades.

It appears to be another message about the end of the world.

The theologian A. J. Conyers said, decades ago, that climate change is the eschatological theme of our age:

> We were becoming, [at the end of the twentieth century], around
> the world, a people with a sense of the apocalypse. We were living
> every day with the apocalyptic dangers of atomic annihilation,
> environmental catastrophes and the abyss of random, widespread
> and even universal destruction. This had never happened before.
> Now we thought not only of our own death but of the possible
> death of humanity.[72]

Talking about the end of the world in 1995, when Conyers wrote the
passage above, there was a spooky similarity to 2020, when this book
was written. End-of-the-world conversations bring on anxiety and fear.
But it doesn't have to be that way. As usual, the Bible offers a different
perspective for everything, including thinking about climate change,
dealing with it, fixing it, and living through it.

In this chapter, we will frame the most pressing issue of our time
within the biblical history of the world. It must start with a story. Our
story. Once upon a time, there was a couple of gardeners who would be
kings. But they failed miserably.

God's creation was created good

There is a myth going around since the Middle Ages saying that God
created the world perfect. But if you look at the Bible, you won't see the
idea of "perfect" in the beginning. You will see "very good". God created
his world and considered it "very good". In the middle of it, he planted
a garden:

> Now the Lord had planted a garden in the East, in Eden; and
> there he put the man he had formed (. . .) The Lord took the man
> and put him in the Garden of Eden to work it and take care of it.
> *Genesis 2:8,15 (NIV)*

So, the Garden of Eden had to be "worked" and "taken care of". Humanity's
first job was that of a gardener–priest who would take care of that sacred,
temple-like space in which he would have a relationship with the creator,

with the living things around and with each other. That is why we feel good closer to nature—that's why we miss it when we live too long in our jungles of brick and mortar. An article from the Food and Agriculture Organization of the United Nations says:

> Research shows that living in close proximity to urban green spaces and having access to them, can improve physical and mental health, for example, by decreasing high blood pressure and stress. This, in turn, contributes to the well-being of urban communities.[73]

The further we distance ourselves from the rest of creation, the more self-centred we become, to the point of arrogance and selfishness.

The other day I (Daniel) was teaching my year 7, eleven-year-old children, a fundamental lesson about diffusion and particle movement. Then, students screamed. There was a spider in the classroom, the giant house spider, *Eratigena atrica*—which is not dangerous at all.

A lot of children wanted to kill the spider, though. But then, one fearless boy decided to get the spider on his hand and save it. He was trying, but the spider was too quick for him. So, I took a beaker, and we trapped the spider inside it. Since that kind of spider cannot climb glasses, he could safely save the spider from eternal demise, bringing the animal to the green outside.

I used that as a lesson to the kids, obviously. That time of the year spiders, which are very good at catching flies that multiply like crazy during summer, go indoors, when the cold looms, to look for a mate. Therefore, that might just have been a spider looking for a girlfriend. How would you feel if you went out one night and then, when you are about to find the person of your dreams, someone stomps on your head?

That only happens because people got arrogant, and forgot we are creatures of God, like any other creature. Instead of respecting them, we crush the animal just because we can. But we must remember we have an extraordinary God-given job. We have got to "work" the creation and "take care of it".

Now, don't get me wrong. While it's true to say that we can save some animals, it is naïve to say that we can save the planet. The earth saves

Figure 25: *Eratigena atrica*, on a dollar bill for size comparison. Believe me, one of those can create a ruckus in a classroom. But why does it go there in the first place?

itself and has done so ever since God created it. The energy that comes from our sun balances out; the species' populations self-regulate and even biomes which were destroyed recover after some time, if we leave them be. Moreover, this is God's world, and he is concerned about it too. Hence, he gave us the job. As gardener-priests, we must tend it, to make life better for us and the rest of God's creation under our responsibility—or to use biblical terminology, "dominion".

But we, humans, have a problem as soon as we see trees with delicious, good-looking fruits.

Humankind's greed is a curse

> When the woman saw that the fruit of the tree was good for food and pleasing to the eye, and also desirable for gaining wisdom, she took some and ate it. She also gave some to her husband who was with her, and he ate it.
>
> [God] said: Because you listened to your wife and ate the fruit from the tree about which I commanded you, "You must not eat from it,"

> Cursed is the ground because of you;
> through painful toil you will eat food from it all the days of your life.
> It will produce thorns and thistles for you,
> and you will eat the plants of the field.
> By the sweat of your brow
> you will eat your food
> until you return to the ground,
> since from it you were taken;
> for dust you are
> and to dust you will return
>
> *Genesis 3:6,17–19 (NIV)*

The story of the Fall needs some revisiting nowadays. Firstly, because it is in the centre of the climate chaos problem; it retells the story of the origin of sin, when God defined what was good and what was evil but humanity, represented by Adam and Eve, got greedy and wanted to redefine good and evil for themselves.[74] Indeed, the serpent only gave them the excuse they were looking for.

Focus on the last part of the story, the curse. Whereas before sin, people would work the garden and take care of it, they would now have to do the same, *but* without nature's cooperation. What else can we expect? God won't be there in the relationship anymore, so how can earth cooperate with the enemy of its creator?

We went from friend to fiend overnight.

What we see from that moment on is a cycle happening every single generation. The human arrogance, pride (a word people cherish nowadays) of defining good and evil by ourselves, without God, has become the standard practice. That is original sin. And, according to Irenaeus, as seen by John Walton, something analogous to the climate chaos we produced:

> In a pollution model, we know well that one person can pollute a stream and everyone downstream suffers; one company can pour in toxic waste and everyone gets cancer; one industry can pollute the air and everyone suffers. When one person makes his or her own interests the centre, that person can create a toxic environment for everyone. In Genesis, the toxic environment involves what we might call "disorder pollution," but as in ecological pollution, all creation groans and disorder reigns. We are all born into that toxic environment, and we all suffer the consequences both universally and particularly, and therefore we are all in need of salvation.[75]

The sad thing about it is not only that Adam and Eve released spiritual pollutants down the spiritual stream, but we keep doing the same ourselves, both spiritually and physically, because the two are connected. It all has to do with what is good for me, without thinking of the others, humans or wildlife. It's selfishness and pride. It's sin.

We experience the dilemma daily. Every time you do your washing up, are you asking whether your soap is biodegradable? Because if it is not, other living things are going to die because of your washing up. Is

"biodegradable" really good or is it overrated? Do you try to reduce the amount of plastic you use in your household? Because if you don't, that plastic ends up in a landfill, or worse, in the ocean, potentially killing animals. Do you practise fly-tipping instead of going to the local recycling centre? Do you carefully separate the rubbish into compostable and recyclable? Because if you don't, your waste will add to that pollution which will affect other people. These are questions demanding an answer, and they boil down into one question.

Are you taking care of God's garden?

An article published in 2019 in *The Guardian* investigates how large clothing stores in the UK make a lot of profit by selling cheap clothes. It turns out there is a cost for the low price we pay.[76] As the wise proverb says, "Nothing is free, because someone is paying for it."

For instance, in 2013, in Bangladesh, the deadliest accident in the history of the garment industry cost many lives. When one of the factories collapsed, 1134 people died. And double that number were injured, some for life, as recorded by Nathan Fitch and Ismail Ferdous in a documentary for the *New York Times'* YouTube channel:

> People don't want to pay more [for their products], so how the producer would pay more to the worker?" said the photojournalist Ismail Ferdous, who reported on the incident. People working in that industry, producing the clothes we use, earn $68 a month when earning the minimum wage, but many factories pay even less.[77]

Figure 26: The Tietê river, one of the biggest rivers in Brazil, running for more than 1000 km, from Salesópolis near the southeast coast, towards the River Paraná, in the countryside. When it crosses the area of Great São Paulo, it receives a lot of pollutants, of all kinds and various sources, including industrial waste and sewage. The process of degradation started probably in 1940 and continues nowadays. The images show its source, in Salesópolis (top), and a dam in Pirapora do Bom Jesus. The white foam is pollution from several cities.

And we are not even considering the problem of cotton, although reporter
Gaby Hinsliff does that:

> Fashion is the second most polluting industry in the world,
> second only to oil, creating environmental headaches right
> through from production to the landfill created when people
> tire of their bargains. . . . Cotton is a thirsty crop, draining water
> resources, while polyester made from oil-based polymers has
> twice its carbon footprint. Deforestation caused by clearing land
> for clothing fibre production risks accelerating global heating.[78]

The Christian must read things like that and ask deeper questions. Have
you ever asked where your lovely, new five-pound T-shirt with that
beautiful stamp of a Bible verse came from? Has the coffee you drink after
the Sunday service been fairly or responsibly traded in poorer countries?

Or are you not bothered?

Climate chaos is the product of our greed, our desire for things,
and our comfortable ignorance. Sadly, our generation's Church has
also participated in things like those for a silly reason: it does not ask
where things come from, partially because of a misunderstanding of
Paul's advice in 1 Corinthians 10:25 (NIV): "Eat anything sold in the
meat market without raising questions of conscience." But that must be
contextualized. In that situation, Paul was talking about knowingly eating
food sacrificed for idols, which would be wrong for Christians to do;
moreover there was unhealthy judgement in the Church on what type
of food should Christians eat. For the situation we are discussing, verses
23 and 24 would apply better:

> "I have the right to do anything", you say—but not everything is
> beneficial. "I have the right to do anything"—but not everything
> is constructive. No one should seek their own good, but the good
> of others. (NIV)

So, we *should* be asking some questions in order to "seek the good of
others". What is the environmental impact of an electricity-rich, plastic-
intense service of a small community such as many churches? What if

it is a megachurch instead? Which communities are impacted by our practices and which people are suffering so that we can have a lovely multimedia service with cheap coffee and biscuits at the end, displaying nice, stamped T-shirts from an exploited country we know nothing about? How often do we ask those questions?

The creation in expectation

> . . . the creation waits in eager expectation for the children of God to be revealed. For the creation was subject to frustration, not by its own choice, but by the will of the one who subjected it, in hope that the creation itself will be liberated from its bondage to decay and brought into the freedom and glory of the children of God.
>
> *Romans 8:19–21 (NIV)*

> . . . if anyone is in Christ, the new creation has come: The old has gone, the new is here! . . . God was reconciling the world to himself in Christ . . .
>
> *2 Corinthians 5:17,19 (NIV)*

In September 2019, millions upon millions of people around the world took to the streets in what they called a Climate Strike. The United Kingdom had witnessed something similar, albeit smaller, earlier in the same year with the Extinction Rebellion protests. But this time around the turnout was incredible. Most of the protestors were children, twelve to seventeen years old, or even younger. Following Greta Thunberg's example, they were expressing fear of the unpredictable but almost undoubtedly gloomy future for the planet. They demanded action and justice from their respective governments.

Temperatures are rising, storms are more frequent, and floods are leading many to leave their homes. According to the Public Broadcasting Service (PBS), the next thirty years will see the forced migration of more than 200 million people due to environmental catastrophes.[79] Some estimates go even higher and suggest one billion people, from countries

Figure 27: One of the global climate strikes that happened in 2019. This one was in Wellington, New Zealand.

becoming either uninhabitable or disappearing due to the rising of sea level. Our generation must prepare for the worst migration crisis ever.

Are we prepared to open our doors to those people?

One country, Kiribati, is already preparing for its demise, and its people are bitter when talking about climate change. For them, the issue is a matter of daily concern. They complain about the inaction of wealthier countries, and the injustice of their own suffering, caused by others in other parts of the world wanting more comfortable lives.[80]

Where are the Christians, though? God's creation is clearly frustrated, people are suffering, but we are, as the singer Keith Green put it, "sleeping in the light". Paul reminds us that it is the freedom and glory of the children of God which will liberate creation from its bondage.

However, sometimes it seems the children of God do not grasp the real dimensions of the sacrifice Christ has made. He not only obtained our salvation and restored our relationship with God. He also reconciled the world to God, so we are free once more to work God's garden and take care of it through his redemption and grace.

At this point, it is useful to recall Jesus' Parable of the Talents. The farm owner went travelling for some time. He gave his servants his money, to be "taken care of". After a long time, he returned and held the servants accountable for the money. Two of them had been faithful and obtained a profit of 100 per cent. One of them, afraid of the owner's reputation, had hidden it and neglected his duty. So, the Lord's valuable resource was wasted.

It is possible to apply the meaning of the parable to one duty which the Church needs to be reminded of: it needs to take care of its Lord's crops. Not only harvesting new Christians but caring for the very soil where those Christians and non-Christians live and on which they rely. When we look to the natural resources with greed, apathy or wilful ignorance, we are sinning, because we are not bothered about God's creation. But he will hold us accountable.

Before the throne we'll have to explain every plastic bottle cluttering up the ocean. He will ask us about the microplastics that are poisoning animals and people. He will recall every insect that we squish without a second thought just because they are annoying or small; he will present every carbon dioxide molecule emitted because we can't be bothered walking short distances. All of this will be shouted from the rooftops.

God's judgement is coming

> And the twenty-four elders, who were seated on their thrones before God, fell on their faces and worshipped God, saying:
>
> "We give thanks to you, Lord God Almighty,
> the One who is and who was,
> because you have taken your great power
> and have begun to reign.
> The nations were angry,
> and your wrath has come.
> The time has come for judging the dead,
> and for rewarding your servants the prophets
> and your people who revere your name,
> both great and small —
> and for destroying those who destroy the earth."
>
> *Revelation 11:16–18 (NIV)*

Everyone agrees that the world is going to end. Either in 5 billion years, when the sun will have burnt all its fuel and will swell up, engulfing Mercury, Venus and the Earth; as we said on page 2, Andromeda could finish us off before that by crashing at our galaxy; or the end will be brought about by an asteroid colliding against our planet someday. A pulsar might hit the Earth from far away in the Universe with a beam of energy, or perhaps nations will engage in a nuclear war. The world will come to an end, eventually. It's not a matter of if; it is a matter of when.

The Book of Revelation talks about this, but it points to that fact from a different point of view. The core idea is Christ returning to judge the living and the dead. It is all about justice. In Chapter 11, it is interesting to note that his judgement will include the destruction of "those who destroy the earth".

We all are going to be there, accountable, in front of the creator who hired us to work his farm. In times where people are desperate for a solution that will save their communities, jobs and lives, will you say "God, I know your reputation, so I decided to hide your resources and shy away from the problem"? Will you show your clothes or phones to God and be prepared to meet the ones who produced your goods? Will you be ashamed to shake their hands? Will you have shared your water with them? Will you have given them your used clothes, or will you see them naked because you tossed your clothes in the bin?

> Then he will say to those on his left, "Depart from me, you cursed, into the eternal fire prepared for the devil and his angels. For I was hungry and you gave me no food, I was thirsty and you gave me no drink, I was a stranger and you did not welcome me, naked and you did not clothe me, sick and in prison, and you did not visit me." Then they also will answer, saying, "Lord, when did we see you hungry or thirsty or a stranger or naked or sick or in prison, and did not minister to you?" Then he will answer them, saying, "Truly, I say to you, as you did not do it to one of the least of these, you did not do it to me."
>
> *Matthew 25:41–45*

God worries about his creation too. He does not like animals going extinct because someone would like to hang their heads as trophies in the living room or eat them as expensive delicacies. He does not approve the killing of rhinos so their horns can be used to produce an aphrodisiac effect. We know this because those creatures are "very good" according to him! Moreover, he is concerned about humanity, so much so that he sent his son to suffer and die for every single one of us. And the knowledge and truth of Jesus redeeming us in this creation can free people from ignorance.

God is not against development. We must expand, grow and multiply, and fill the earth. But responsibly, growing our cities in harmony with the creation we are part of. That is possible when we acknowledge the value of the world around us and how connected with it we are. When we gaze at the dust in the soil and see our family trees go all the way back to it.

How to stop climate change

We are going to live through rough days ahead with climate change. The main cause is human activity, and sin is a big part of the equation. With our greed and sin, ignorance and lust, we are making everything worse.

However, our story does not end at the end of the world. God values his creation very much and wants it to be "very good" again but this time with the gardeners as true kings:

> Then the angel showed me the river of the water of life, as clear as crystal, flowing from the throne of God and of the Lamb down the middle of the great street of the city. On each side of the river stood the tree of life, bearing twelve crops of fruit, yielding its fruit every month. And the leaves of the tree are for the healing of the nations. No longer will there be any curse. The throne of God and of the Lamb will be in the city, and his servants will serve him. (. . .) And they will reign for ever and ever.
>
> *Revelation 22:1–5 (NIV)*

I love the picture of the holy city and the holy garden together in the presence of God. Redemption is everywhere in the end. And there will not be any curse. We will, truly, live happily ever after.

We might have failed as gardeners but there is still hope. To stop climate change, one must stop sin. Yet, no one can do that but Jesus Christ, who conquered sin on the cross. It turns out then that he is the solution for climate change, as well as the solution for everything else—including your own life of bad habits and sin. Repent, and your sin will be dealt with. In the process of getting to know Jesus better, you will also reduce your carbon footprint because you will see the world differently—the work of art your Father created, with you in it. As Francis Schaeffer puts it:

> God treats His creation with integrity: each thing in its own order, each thing the way He made it. If God treats His creation in that way, should we not treat our fellow-creatures with similar integrity? If God treats the tree like a tree, the machine like a

machine, the man like a man, shouldn't I, as a fellow-creature, do the same—treating each thing in integrity in its own order? And for the highest reason: because I love God—I love the One who has made it! Loving the Lover who has made it, I have respect for the thing He has made.[81]

Epilogue

And there was a woman who had had a discharge of blood for
twelve years, and who had suffered much under many physicians,
and had spent all that she had, and was no better but rather grew
worse. She had heard the reports about Jesus and came up behind
him in the crowd and touched his garment. For she said, "If I
touch even his garments, I will be made well." And immediately
the flow of blood dried up, and she felt in her body that she
was healed of her disease. (. . .) And he said to her, "Daughter,
your faith has made you well; go in peace, and be healed of your
disease."

Mark 5:25–29,34

Nobody was prepared for a pandemic like COVID-19. The new type
of coronavirus that hit the world in December 2019 wreaked havoc in
people's lives, economies and health systems around the world. It has also
put some things into perspective for everyone.

Firstly, there were the numbers, graphs, tables, models and predictions
scientists were putting forward to inform policies and strategies. The
scenarios were grim, and there was little hope that death rates would
be low. One prediction, based on the infection rate of the pathogen
being equal to 2.5 (the number called R, that is, one person infecting 2.5
people in five days, generating 406 cases per month), stated that would
lead to up to 7 billion infections and 40 million deaths without public
intervention.[82] Many countries ordered "lockdowns" to prevent the virus
from spreading.

And so, our generation was forced to face the reality of our mortality,
since we all could get a deadly virus just by going outside.

But the second thing that the novel coronavirus (technically named
SARS-CoV-2) put into perspective was the fear of economic collapse,

unemployment and death. The general anxiety grew as much as the pandemic did, and fear was occupying the shelves of every stripped-empty food store. The worst of people was seen, with selfishness and judgement prevailing in some. But in others, the best was seen, in the form of altruistic acts (in England, 750,000 people volunteered to help the National Health Service) and in the form of personal sacrifice (such as staff keeping some nurseries open to care for the children of nurses, doctors and delivery drivers). Individual examples were many, such as the priest Giuseppe Berardelli, aged seventy-two, who declined the use of a respirator bought for him by his parishioners, so an unknown younger patient could survive. He died soon afterwards.[83]

And so, our generation was forced to face the illusion of control over our lives, since it didn't matter how well we followed guidelines—there was always a risk looming.

While preparing this book for publication, these horrible events almost turned into a personal case study of the central idea proposed in this book. As we asserted in Chapter 2, science and faith can work together to help us explain and deal with the world we live in.

In a Church of England school, the Bible verse chosen for that year, long before any coronavirus hit the news, was "Give all your worries and cares to God, for he cares about you" (1 Peter 5:7, NLT). As we saw school and church closures, as we ended up meeting our communities via social media and video calls through the technological wonder that is the internet, the message kept being reinforced. Social distancing became the phrase of the day, quickly transforming from jest to judgement, allowing us to worry about the most vulnerable people or to frown at pedestrians we knew nothing about.

Yet, science kept only providing numbers, scenarios and predictions. The world was desperate for a vaccine, a remedy. Without any of those, and in need of confronting our fears and thoughts in our self-isolation, many of us turned to God and his healing power, as we waited for the worst to pass.

We are not different from that unknown woman from the Gospel of Mark, after all. She had a disease, like many others. Contrary to the belief of many contemporary Christians, her story teaches us that we are going to get ill, experience traumas and troubles, and that some of us will die from these things. We are certainly not immune to suffering as we argued in Chapter 3. Although the diseases vary greatly, and our pain with them, God's care is constant.

Pandemics seem to start out of nowhere, although there is always a beginning. In December 2019, news about the first cases of COVID-19 in China reached the UK. Many people thought it was just another type of flu. Just another virus, far away in the world, that would hijack somebody else's cell machinery to produce copies of itself—a protein case enveloping an RNA strand. Until a case popped up in Italy, and then more. Soon, the US, South Korea, and Iran reported an increasing number of cases. It started to feel like it was "coming", and then one day it arrived in the UK, always closer to our cities.

After a month from the first reports, thousands of cases were being presented daily on government briefings on television. The government asserted that they were guided by scientists' modelling and advice. New information was published by Imperial College London and other organizations.[84] Just one week later Prime Minister Boris Johnson announced a "lockdown". Less than a week after that, a quarter of the population of the world was confined to their homes to delay the spread of the virus and suppress its growth, so that public health systems would not be overwhelmed.

Again, fear itself was infectious. People started panicking. They bought more and more goods from the supermarkets. Sometimes shelves were emptied in less than ten minutes from replenishing. Toilet paper, for some reason, was the chief product hoarded by people. Some countries, like Brazil, lacking a plan and leadership to tackle a health crisis, also felt political instability amidst hundreds of thousands of deaths and jobs lost.

Interestingly, after some months the world started to realize that lockdowns were beginning to have a positive impact on climate chaos too, since fewer factories and cars were operating, and the emissions of CO_2 rapidly decreased.[85] (But, as we saw in Chapter 6, there were expressions of selfishness such as hoarding of food or holding "COVID parties".)

Although science was doing its job, by predicting, describing, explaining, and producing medicine, this was not enough to calm people down. We were terrified, despite science allowing countries to suppress the disease and "flatten the curve". The world was waiting for a vaccine as if that would be our saviour, our chemical messiah. However, science has its limits, or it just gets there too late. On this occasion, it was late for thousands of people worldwide, who died, many of them alone, not able to see their loved ones before their time came.

Within the church, Christians from all denominations started meeting together through video conference, and every day we prayed for people. Some volunteered to help. By just doing our jobs more conscientiously, or staying at home, we went beyond the call of duty. Some offered financial help, some simply offered chatting through the internet. The best in people came out. In acts of kindness and sacrifice, in common grace, Jesus was heard of, and seen, over and over again. We saw a glimpse of what spiritual gardening looks like, caring for the seed God had planted, fulfilling our true purpose in creation (see Chapter 5). The Spirit of God was hovering over the chaotic waters.

But those stories were only reports about Christians. People might have believed them, or not. To feel their power, one has to approach Christ himself and interact with him. This is what the relationship between Christianity and science is really about; through doctors, scientists, nurses, data, vaccines and ventilators, God was helping. He was teaching, amid anxiety and fear, that, as Psalm 46 teaches, he may bring desolation to the world, but also peace. In this process, though, as we learned in Chapter 4, we are never, ever, alone. Pastor John Piper put it quite well in a podcast:

> The coronavirus is a wake-up question to the world, especially Christians: Is your life a confirmation that God has called you out of darkness into his marvellous light? These are the people—the called and the lovers of God—who have a warrant, a ground, a foundation in reality not to be afraid, but to be steadied by unshakable peace.[86]

Science offers numbers, natural explanation, and practical solutions. It states we will die; it describes symptoms, it produces solutions sometimes. The Christian faith offers a worldview, one that can lead to joy in the middle of chaos and pandemics; it reminds us that death is not the end; God is reigning, calming our anxiety. These perspectives are not at odds with each other. On the contrary, they complement each other quite well. Christianity shakes the ground of any person who gives it a chance. It forces a new way of looking at the numbers and statistics science provides. Numbers do not die. Brothers and sisters die. People who suffer die. Their families are left heartbroken. When you cannot do anything for them, you "weep with those who weep". As Rosaria Butterfield puts it, "conversion can be a train wreck".[87] But it is also a blessing.

Christ changes everything.

Christianity does not despise the scientific data. On the contrary, many faithful Christians serve through production and analysis of that scientific data. But the data is mute, amoral, insensitive, and raw. Christians might be horrified by the numbers, but they turn their eyes upon Jesus, and the light that comes from him is more powerful and brighter than the stars we talked about in Chapter 1; he makes the things of our world to "grow strangely dim", as the hymn puts it.

The Triune God's power is a powerful lens that converges and focuses what we see into a clearer image of reality, enriching it. The woman in Mark experienced that when Jesus healed her. In her case though, there was more than healing. Christ did something else for her. He used her disease to help her understand and believe in God in a way that she had never tried before. Jesus eliminated the fear the doctors could not.

Science explains fear, and even treats it. But it does not eliminate its source. It does not reframe fear into a new way of seeing the world. However, the faith in Jesus does precisely that. In the podcast mentioned above, John Piper says:

> What God is doing — among a million other things — in the coronavirus, is forcing the issue of reality. And one of the litmus tests of whether your life is based on reality or based on the mirage of God-ignoring pillars, holding up the cultural temple of secularism, is fear. The test of the foundations of your life is fear. Oh, what a precious gift God is giving to us to discover, while we still have time, that the pillars holding up our peace are hollow and made of papier mâché. That's a gift.[88]

Conclusion

In the minds of many people a person can either be a scientist or a Christian, as if they were born in a certain country and could only emigrate from one to another, never to return. If that were the case, the world would be full of people who don't understand either, living in a nostalgic loneliness, thus, engaging in a cold war of worldviews, producing misunderstanding, harming people and seeing dissidents in both sides. Not different from ours, is it?

But through this book we saw that there is no need for that approach, and we can certainly have dual citizenship. If science and faith were different countries, they would be connected by a bridge called worship, where many people would spend hours gazing at the sunrise, starwatching, having peaceful conversations and celebrating their differences, smiling at the cultural exchange and the skies proclaiming the works of God's hands.

One day, Jesus went to Samaria. An outcast woman engaged in a conversation with him, questioning him about the right place to worship God, whether it was in Jerusalem, within the temple, or in Samaria, on a mountain. He answered:

> . . . a time is coming and has now come when the true worshipers will worship the Father in Spirit and in truth, for they are the kind of worshipers the Father seeks.
>
> *John 4:23 (NIV)*

The Christian worshiping on the pew
rejoices in the laboratory
The scientist humming at the microscope
sings out loud in the church
The minister and the scientist
offer each other a sign of peace
As the Bible and the Science Book
are read together
As scientific knowledge and worship
are fuelled by Wonder
Under the proclaiming skies
made by the Creator's love
revealed in a cross of wood
described by a humble neurone
Amen.

Image sources

Figure 1: Rachael Ayers, *Abraham's Sky*, 2021.

Figure 2: Andromeda Galaxy, Isaac Roberts, 1899. <https://commons. wikimedia.org/wiki/File:Pic_iroberts1.jpg>, accessed 10 June 2021.

Figure 3: The Periodic Table of Elements, as of 2020. <https:// commons.wikimedia.org/wiki/File:Simple_Periodic_Table_ Chart-en.svg>, accessed 10 June 2021.

Figure 4: Spiral Galaxy M51. <https://commons.wikimedia.org/wiki/ File:2019abn_NBO_2019-03-12.png>, accessed 10 June 2021.

Figure 5: M51 Whirlpool Galaxy Black Hole. <http://hubblesite.org/ image/68/news_release/1992-17>, accessed 10 June 2021.

Figure 6: Rachael Ayers, *Ben Nevis*, 2021.

Figure 7: James Irwin and the Lunar Roving Vehicle during the Apollo 15 mission. <https://commons.wikimedia.org/wiki/File:Apollo_15_ Lunar_Rover_and_Irwin.jpg>, accessed 10 June 2021.

Figure 8: Human embryo seven weeks after conception. The Czerwiakowski Gynaecological and Obstetrics Hospital, Krakow, Poland. <https://commons.wikimedia.org/wiki/File:Embryo_7_ weeks_after_conception.jpg>, accessed 10 June 2021.

Figure 9: Khelvi Marques, *Two climbers*, 2021.

Figure 10: George Bouverie Goddard, *The struggle for existence*,1879. <https://commons.wikimedia.org/wiki/File:George_Bouverie_ Goddard04a.jpg>, accessed 10 June 2021.

Figure 11: John Gould, Darwin's finches, before 1882. <https:// commons.wikimedia.org/wiki/File:Darwin%27s_finches_by_ Gould.jpg>, accessed 10 June 2021.

Figure 12: *Dugesia subtentaculata*. picture by Edward Solà (2008). <https://commons.wikimedia.org/wiki/File:Dugesia_ subtentaculata_1.jpg>, accessed 10 June 2021.

Figure 13: *Biston betullaria*, taken by Daniel Ruy Pereira in the Manchester Museum.

Figure 14: Nicolas Colombel, *Christ healing the blind*, 1682. <https://en.wikipedia.org/wiki/Healing_the_man_blind_from_birth#/media/File:Nicolas_Colombel_-_Christ_Healing_the_Blind.jpg>, accessed 10 June 2021.

Figure 15: Very Large Array radio telescopes. Image courtesy of: National Science Foundation. <https://www.nsf.gov/news/mmg/media/images/star2_h.jpg>, accessed 10 June 2021.

Figure 16: Hans Bernhard, *Egyptian goddess Nut*, 1976. <https://commons.wikimedia.org/wiki/File:Goddess_Nut_2.JPG>, accessed 10 June 2021.

Figure 17: William Anders, *Earthrise*, 1968. <https://commons.wikimedia.org/wiki/File:NASA-Apollo8-Dec24-Earthrise.jpg>, accessed 10 June 2021.

Figure 18: Hubble Ultra Violet Deep Field, negative filter. NASA/ESA, 2018. <https://commons.wikimedia.org/wiki/File:NASA-Galaxies15k-HubbleHDUV-20180816.png>, accessed 10 June 2021.

Figure 19: ALH84001. NASA, 2018. <https://commons.wikimedia.org/wiki/File:ALH84001.jpg>, accessed 10 June 2021.

Figure 20: The Sounds of Earth. NASA/JPL. <https://commons.wikimedia.org/wiki/File:The_Sounds_of_Earth_Record_Cover_-_GPN-2000-001978.jpg>, accessed 10 June 2021.

Figure 21: Lioness vs Cape Buffalo. <https://commons.wikimedia.org/wiki/File:Lioness_vs_Cape_Buffalo_(cropped).jpg>, accessed 10 June 2021.

Figure 22: Rachael Ayers, *Hebrew cosmogony*, 2020.

Figure 23. Ptah, the Lord of Order, from a Memphis Egyptian creation myth. <https://commons.wikimedia.org/wiki/File:Ptah_(1885)_-_TIMEA.jpg>, accessed 10 June 2021.

Figure 24: L. Gruner, *Chaos Monster and Sun God*, 1853. <https://commons.wikimedia.org/wiki/File:Chaos_Monster_and_Sun_God.png>, accessed 10 June 2021.

Figure 25: *Eratrigena attica*, under former taxonomic name *T.duellica*. <https://commons.wikimedia.org/wiki/File:Tegenaria_duellica_and_dollar_bill.JPG>, accessed 10 June 2021.

Figure 26: Daniel Santiago, *Nascente do rio Tietê*, 2008. <https://upload. wikimedia.org/wikipedia/commons/thumb/f/f1/Nascente_do_ Tiete.jpg/1200px-Nascente_do_Tiete.jpg>, and <https://commons. wikimedia.org/wiki/File:Barragem_de_Pirapora_do_Bom_Jesus. jpg>, accessed 10 June 2021.

Figure 27: Young people in the School Strike for Climate in Wellington, New Zealand., by David Tong, 2019, <https://commons.wikimedia. org/wiki/File:School_Strike_for_Climate_in_Wellington_13.jpg>, accessed 10 June 2021.

Notes

1   Origen, *On First Principles*, Book 4, 1.16.

2   Thomas Aquinas, *Summa Theologica*, Question 74.

3   Albert Einstein, *The World as I see it*. Retrieved from: <https://history.aip.org/history/exhibits/einstein/essay.htm>.

4   William Bragg, in Sir Kerr Grant, *The Life and Works of Sir William Bragg*, 1952, p. 43. <https://todayinsci.com/B/Bragg_William/BraggWilliam-Quotations.htm>, accessed 15 September 2020.

5   *Cultural Backgrounds Study Bible* (Grand Rapids, MI: Zondervan, 2016), p. xxxii.

6   From the European Space Agency's website, <http://www.esa.int/Science_Exploration/Space_Science/Herschel/How_many_stars_are_there_in_the_Universe>, accessed 25 October 2020.

7   Martin Rees, *Just Six Numbers* (London: Weidenfeld & Nicolson, 1999), p. 82.

8   Brendan B. Larsen et al., "Inordinate Fondness Multiplied and Redistributed: the Number of Species on Earth and the New Pie of Life", *The Quarterly Review of Biology* 92:3 (September 2017).

9   Rees, *Just Six Numbers*, pp. 49–50.

10   Sadhu Sundar Singh, *At the Master's Feet* Kindle Edition (New York: Start Publishing LLC, n. d.), pp. 13–14.

11   Justo L. González, *Creation: The Apple of God's Eye* (Nashville, TN: Abingdon Press, 2015), pp. 18–20.

12   González, *Creation*, pp. 18–20.

13   Shelby Lorman, *Neil deGrasse Tyson on the Power of Curiosity*, <https://thriveglobal.com/stories/neil-degrasse-tyson-on-the-power-of-curiosity/>, accessed 18 September 2020.

14   Alister McGrath, *A Fine-tuned Universe* (Louisville, KY: Westminster John Knox Press, 2009), pp. 52–82.

15   Alister McGrath, *Enriching Our Vision of Reality* (London: SPCK, 2016), p. 6.

16   Francis Collins, *The Language of God* (London: Pocket Books, 2007), p. 93.

[17] Stuart K. Hine, "How Great Thou Art", 1949.

[18] McGrath, *A Fine-tuned Universe*, p. 6.

[19] This story is based on the analogy of the mountain by Charles A. Coulson in *Science and Christian Belief* (London: Oxford University Press, 1955).

[20] As quoted in Clifford Pickover, *Archimedes to Hawking* (Oxford: Oxford University Press, 2008), p. 7.

[21] <https://aleteia.org/2017/11/10/louis-pasteur-father-of-microbiology-and-a-catholic/>, accessed 18 September 2020.

[22] Steven J. Lawson, <https://www.sermonaudio.com/sermoninfo.asp?SID=1124101529370>, accessed 18 September 2020.

[23] Carl Sagan, *The Demon-Haunted World: Science as a Candle in the Dark* (New York: Ballantine Books, 1997).

[24] John Polkinghorne, *The Way the World Is: The Christian Perspective of a Scientist* (London: SPCK, 1983), p. 112.

[25] Ernst Mayr, *This is Biology: The Science of the Living World* (London: Belknap Press, 1997), p. 27.

[26] McGrath, *A Fine-tuned Universe*, p. 69.

[27] Max Planck, *Where is Science Going?* (London: G. Allen & Unwin, 1933), p. 169.

[28] <https://www.nasa.gov/mission_pages/apollo/missions/apollo15.html>, accessed 27 October 2020.

[29] Carl C. Gaither and Alma E. Cavazos-Gaither, *Gaither's Dictionary of Scientific Quotations*, 2nd edn (New York: Springer, 2012), p. 1789.

[30] Jamie A. Davies, *Life Unfolding: How the Human Body Creates Itself* (Oxford: Oxford University Press, 2014), p. 259.

[31] Stuart K. Hine, "How Great Thou Art", 1949.

[32] C. S. Lewis, *The Problem of Pain* (San Francisco: Harper San Francisco, 2001 [1940]), p. 91.

[33] C. S. Lewis, *A Grief Observed* (London: Faber & Faber, 2013).

[34] As quoted in Eric Russert Kraemer, "Darwin's doubts and the problems of animal pain", p. 3. *Between the Species* II August 2002 <https://digitalcommons.calpoly.edu/bts/>, accessed 18 September 2020.

[35] Denis Alexander, *Creation or Evolution: Do We Have to Choose?* (Oxford: Monarch, 2008).

[36] Charles Darwin, *On the Origin of Species*, 6th edition, 1883.

[37] Ronald E. Osborn, *Death Before the Fall* (Downers Grove: InterVarsity Press, 2014), p. 154.

38 William Cowper, "God moves in a mysterious way", in *The Olney Hymns*, 1773.

39 O. M. Arenas, E. E. Zaharieva, A. Para et al., "Activation of planarian TRPA1 by reactive oxygen species reveals a conserved mechanism for animal nociception." *Nature Neuroscience* 20 (2017), pp. 1686–93.

40 Neil Andrews, "A flatworm to the rescue", 7 November 2017, *Pain Research Forum.org*. <https://www.painresearchforum.org/news/88483-flatworm-rescue>, accessed 18 September 2020.

41 Alexander, *Creation or Evolution*, pp. 338–9.

42 Osborn, *Death Before the Fall*, p. 159.

43 Lewis, *A Grief Observed*, p. 36.

44 Carl Sagan, *Contact: A novel* (London: Arrow, 1987).

45 Quoted in David Wilkinson, *Science, Religion, and the Search for Extraterrestrial Intelligence* (Oxford: Oxford University Press, 2013), p. 17.

46 "The Search in General". <http://seti.berkeley.edu/FAQ.html#q1>, accessed 30 October 2020. See also Stephen J. Garber, "Searching for good science: The cancellation of NASA's SETI program" *Journal of British Interplanetary Society* 52 (1999), pp.3–12.

47 Wilkinson, *Science, Religion*, pp. 89–90.

48 Arthur C. Clarke, quoted in Michio Kaku, *Visions: How Science Will Revolutionize the Twenty-First Century* (Oxford: Oxford University Press, 1998), p. 295.

49 Roy F. Baumeister and Mark R. Leary, "The need to belong: desire for interpersonal attachments as a fundamental human motivation", *Psychological Bulletin* 117:3 (1995), pp. 497–529, here at p. 522.

50 In this section we depend heavily on the commentaries on Psalm 8 and 19, presented in *NIV Cultural Backgrounds Study Bible* (Grand Rapids: Zondervan, 2016), pp. 886, 895.

51 Artemis Plan: NASA's lunar exploration programme overview, September 2020. For a comprehensive list of missions, their space agencies and their status, see <https://en.wikipedia.org/wiki/List_of_Solar_System_probes>, accessed 18 September 2020.

52 David Hughes, quoted in Wilkinson, *Science, Religion*, p. 85.

53 Wilkinson, *Science, Religion*, p. 136.

54 *Pensées*, quoted in Wilkinson, Science, Religion, p. 141.

55 John Gribbin, *Alone in the Universe: Why Our Planet is Unique* (Chichester: Wiley, 2011), p. xiv.

56 C. Westermann, quoted in Wilkinson, *Science, Religion*, p. 145.

57 Robert Zemeckis, *Contact*, 1997.

58 Quoted in Wilkinson, *Science, Religion*, p. 142.

59 Which are Genesis 1:1–2:3; Genesis 2:4–3:24; Job 38–41; Psalm 104; Proverbs 8:22–31; Ecclesiastes 1:2–11, 12:1–7; and some excerpts of Isaiah 40–55. The list is from William P. Brown, *The Seven Pillars of Creation: The Bible, Science and the Ecology of Wonder* (Oxford: Oxford University Press, 2010), p. 6.

60 John Walton, *The Lost World of Genesis One: Ancient Cosmology and the Origins Debate* (InterVarsity Press, 2010).

61 Walton, *Lost World of Genesis One*, p. 20.

62 This section, in Brown, *Seven Pillars of Creation*, pp. 21–31.

63 See, for example, Tremper Longman III, *Who wrote the Book of Genesis?* Video available at <https://www.youtube.com/watch?v=5vm6QB7jvPQ>, accessed 1 November 2020.

64 Walton, *Lost World of Genesis One*, p. 26.

65 Brown, *Seven Pillars*, p. 37.

66 William P. Brown, " 'Let there be Light!': The Genesis of Biblical Cosmology", *Journal of Cosmology* 9 (2010), pp. 2187–93, <http://journalofcosmology.com/AncientAstronomy111.html>, accessed 18 September 2020.

67 Zachariah Zienka, "What does it mean to be human?" <https://thebibleproject.com/blog/what-does-it-mean-to-be-human/>, accessed 18 September 2020.

68 González, *Creation*, p. 84.

69 Osborn, *Death Before the Fall*, chapter 7.

70 González, *Creation*, p. 79.

71 <https://extinctionrebellion.uk/the-truth/about-us/>, accessed 20 October 2020.

72 A. J. Conyers, *The End: What Jesus Really Said about the Last Things* (Downers Grove: InterVarsity Press, 1995), p. 21.

73 "Building greener cities: nine benefits of urban trees", *Food and Agriculture Organization of the United Nations*, 30 November 2016, <http://www.fao.org/zhc/detail-events/en/c/454543/>, accessed 18 September 2020.

74 Tim Mackie and Jon Collins, "Image of God", video, *The Bible Project*, <https://bibleproject.com/explore/image-god/>, accessed 18 September 2020.

75 John H. Walton, *The Lost World of Adam and Eve* (Downers Grove: InterVarsity Press, 2015), p. 158.

76 Gaby Hinsliff, "Cheap and cheerful: why there's more to Primark's success than you thought", *The Guardian*, 28 May 2019, <https://www.theguardian.>

com/business/2019/may/28/more-to-primark-success-than-you-thought>, accessed 18 September 2020.

77   Nathan Fitch & Ismail Ferdous, "The Deadly Cost of Fashion", *New York Times*, video, <https://www.youtube.com/watch?v=9Fkhzdc4ybw>, accessed 18 September 2020.

78   Hinsliff, "Cheap and cheerful".

79   *Climate Change Will Make MILLIONS Homeless. Where Will They Go?*, PBS Digital Studios, <https://www.youtube.com/watch?v=5xuZT7VkjVg>, accessed 18 September 2020.

80   "People urgently fleeing climate crisis cannot be sent home, UN rules", 20 January 2020. <https://www.bbc.co.uk/news/world-asia-51179931>, accessed 1 June 2021.

81   Francis A. Schaeffer, *Pollution and the Death of Man* (Cambridge: Tyndale House Publishers, 1970), pp. 57–8.

82   Patrick G. T. Walker et al., "Report 12: The Global Impact of COVID-19 and Strategies for Mitigation and Suppression", Imperial College COVID-19 Response Team, 26 March 2020.

83   Aila Slisco, "72-year-old Italian priest who gave his ventilator to younger patient dies of coronavirus", *Newsweek*, 23 March 2020, <https://www.newsweek.com/72-year-old-italian-priest-who-gave-his-ventilator-younger-patient-dies-coronavirus-1493868>, accessed 18 September 2020.

84   Neil M. Ferguson et al., "Impact of non-pharmaceutical interventions (NPIs) to reduce COVID-19 mortality and healthcare demand", Imperial College COVID-19 Response Team, 16 March 2020.

85   Benjamin Storrow, "Global CO2 Emissions Saw Record Drop During Pandemic Lockdown", *Scientific American*, 20 May 2020, <https://www.scientificamerican.com/article/global-co2-emissions-saw-record-drop-during-pandemic-lockdown/>, accessed 18 September 2020.

86   John Piper, in *Ask Pastor John: How do I fight my coronavirus fears?*, 26 March 2020, <https://www.desiringgod.org/interviews/how-do-i-fight-my-coronavirus-fears>, accessed 18 September 2020.

87   Rosaria Champagne Butterfield, "My Train Wreck Conversion", 2013 at <https://www.christianitytoday.com/ct/2013/january-february/my-train-wreck-conversion.html>.

88   John Piper, *Ask Pastor John*.